THE
STRANGE CRITICAL FORTUNES
OF
SHAKESPEARE'S *TIMON OF ATHENS*

Timon on Fortune's "high and pleasant hill"
(I.i) and his "low grave." (V.iv)

From Vol. III of Gulian C. Verplanck's edition of *Shakespeare's Plays* (New York, 1847). Folger Shakespeare Library.

THE

STRANGE CRITICAL FORTUNES

OF

SHAKESPEARE'S *TIMON OF ATHENS*

BY

FRANCELIA BUTLER

The Iowa State University Press, Ames, Iowa, U.S.A.

1966

About the Author:

FRANCELIA BUTLER is assistant professor of English, University of Connecticut. She was formerly on the faculty of the University of Tennessee. She is a graduate of Oberlin College and has obtained the M.A. from Georgetown University and the Ph.D. from the University of Virginia.

Besides this book, she is author of *The Skip Rope Book* (a collection of skipping rhymes for children) and several articles for publications in the fields of medical history and English literature. She is working on another collection of rhymes as well as a book in the area of seventeenth-century drama. She has held a post-doctoral fellowship to the Institute of Medieval and Renaissance Studies at the University of North Carolina, and will work in Lebanon in 1966 on a Fulbright-Hays award.

Mrs. Butler is noted for sponsoring parties for her colleagues with appropriate eighteenth-century cuisine—from savories to snuff—accompanied by the music of Handel, Mozart, Haydn, and Bach. This interest grew partially from Mrs. Butler's study at the Cordon Bleu in Paris where she was also drama critic on the *Paris Herald.* Her sponsorship of other literary activities in connection with the eighteenth century has been recognized by the *Johnsonian Newsletter.*

© 1966 The Iowa State University Press
All rights reserved. Printed in the U.S.A.
First edition, 1966

Library of Congress Catalog Card Number: 65–22377

To my Mother
GRACE WILLIAMS MCWILLIAMS

CONTENTS

FOREWORD

Part One
STRUCTURE
I LORD TIMON'S FRAME: *The Early Editors*   3
II MEAN EYES: *The Divided-Authorship
Theory*   12
III "TIMON" IN THE WOODS: *The
Fragmentation of the Play*   26
IV "TIMON" IN CHAOS: *The "Unfinished"
Theory*   44
V ON FORTUNE'S MOUNT: Timon *and
Defenders of Its Structure*   59

Part Two
MEANING
VI NOBLE TIMON: *Classical and Romantic
Studies*   75
VII LIVELIER THAN LIFE: *Imagery and
"Thematic" Studies*   94

Part Three

TIMON AS A STAGE PLAY

VIII An Empty Coffer: *Structure and Meaning
to the Audience* 119

Part Four

SYNTHESIS

IX Epitaph: *The Synthesis of Structure and
Meaning* 153

Part Five

APPENDICES

A. Sources 161
B. Dating 170
   Bibliography 174
   Index 183

FOREWORD

ROBABLY less is known about *Timon of Athens*
than about any of Shakespeare's plays. Criticism
of the play by scholars is often confused; by lay-
men often deplorably inaccurate or trivial. When in
The Family Shakespeare, Dr. Thomas Bowdler cut the
two whores out of the play, he was taking an unnecessary precaution to omit what "cannot with propriety be
read in a family." Families seem to have left *Timon* un-
thumbed.

My purpose here is to go beyond the mere reputation study—to analyze the critical assumptions under-
lying attitudes toward the play and to suggest the significance of any findings relevant to Shakespeare criticism as a whole.

From this survey of a large body of critical conjecture in historical sequence, it is hoped that certain fresh
observations about *Timon* will emerge, ideas which
might be warped or even lost in a partial examination
of critical comment. But even such a survey must have
its limitations. Although *Timon* is generally accounted

an unpopular play, an enormous amount of criticism has been written about it, largely because it is Shakespeare's. The major critical interest in *Timon* has been in its structure. Therefore this study will begin with the type of textual criticism—the early attempts to divide *Timon* into acts—which tended to draw attention to certain structural difficulties and thus cause later critics to begin investigations of the play with studies of its structure. After this review of structural criticism, I have considered the much smaller body of criticism of the meaning of the play.

By "structure," I mean the interrelation of the parts of the play as dominated by the general character of the whole. By "meaning," I have in mind the dominant ideas conveyed by *Timon,* either through characterization or basic themes.

Most critics of *Timon* consider the structure to be poor. They assign the same major reasons for the poor structure: that the play lacks coherence between scenes. Critics agree generally on what scenes constitute the weak links in the plot. But the explanations offered for this lack of coherence vary widely. Critical opinions are grouped here in accordance with the explanations advanced for the structural defects: (1) no explanation offered, or, corruption of the play by the printers of the Folio of 1623, or, poor writing on Shakespeare's part; (2) incoherences explained on the basis of two or more authors involved in writing the play—two chapters will be devoted to this theory which was developed to an extreme point; (3) postulations that the play was left unfinished: either for unknown reasons, or because Shakespeare saw he had made a poor choice of subjects, or had had a mental illness, or had died.

A few critics have defended the structure on the grounds that the play has either (1) the traditional unity of action or (2) organic unity—that is, that the structure is shaped by a central idea. Those who find organic unity in the play include critics of the Romantic period interested in the character of *Timon* as a study of idealism, and critics of the mid-twentieth century who see the play as an experimental form designed to convey a theme or themes to an intellectual (possibly an Inns-of-Court) audience.

As to meaning, a critic may be interested in a few lines or a particular subject—criticism of a fragmentary nature—or, he may be interested in the characterization of a major figure, and, through this figure, in the thematic idea of the entire play. Critics interested only in portions of the play—"Beauties" or social, aesthetic, or historical insights—are interested in *Timon* primarily as a source of information rather than as a work of literature. I have limited my review of the criticism of meaning primarily to those critics concerned with ideas conveyed in *Timon* through characterization or major themes.

In the synthesis of the opinions of structure and meaning, comparisons have been made as to how critics primarily interested in structure feel about the meaning, and how critics primarily interested in meaning feel about the structure, and from this review, an attempt has been made to arrive at a balanced judgment of *Timon* as a work of literature.

Timon has been performed both by traditional and academic groups. I have reviewed the reactions of audiences to these performances and have made an attempt to arrive at a balanced judgment of *Timon* as a stage play. I have compared the critical experiences with *Timon* as a stage play and as a literary work, the intent being to further the process of arriving at a more definitive critical estimate of the play.

In evaluating the critical reputation of *Timon,* I
intend to extend this study to include scholarly con-
troversies about the transmission of the text, authorship, and staging. I hope that my work will stimulate
a larger study of the plays of Shakespeare the structures
of which have been extensively investigated, such as
the two other plays derived from Plutarch which first
appeared in the Folio of 1623, which also were possibly
in Shakespeare's holograph: *Antony and Cleopatra* and
Coriolanus.

Unless otherwise specified, act and scene divisions
and line numbers will follow those in the Globe edition
of Clark and Wright (1864), the first numbered text.
Unless quoted from a specified text, however, the word-
ing and spelling of quotations will follow the Folio of
1623.

I wish here to acknowledge the kind suggestions of
Professors Fredson Bowers and Lester Beaurline of the
University of Virginia, who directed the dissertation on
which this book is based. I also wish to acknowledge
the cooperation of the staffs of the University Libraries
of Connecticut, Georgetown, Tennessee, and Virginia,
and the Folger Shakespeare Library.

Another important acknowledgment is made to Jan
Bakker, instructor in English at the University of Tennessee, who spent several days at the Folger Shakespeare
Library making the careful selection of historical illus-
trations for the text and who also created the drawing
on the dust jacket.

The logical mind of Professor Mary Ann Mac-
dougall, Director of the Bureau of Statistics at the University of Virginia, helped me to see how I could best
convey my conclusions about *Timon.* Thanks also to

Professors Barbara and William Rosen of the University of Connecticut who supplied data on recent performances of *Timon* in England. The exacting task of preparing the Chart of Ascriptions of Acts and Scenes in Divided Authorship was performed by Mrs. Carol Boykin of the English Department of the University of Tennessee. The final manuscript was typed by Mrs. Mary Alice White.

Much verification of research was done while I was a Fellow at the Southeastern Institute of Medieval-Renaissance Studies, sponsored jointly by the University of North Carolina and Duke University under a grant from the Ford Foundation. For access to the research facilities of these institutions I am deeply grateful.

Especially, I wish to convey my appreciation to the staff, and to Mrs. Rowena G. James, Managing Editor, the Iowa State University Press, for preparing the text for publication.

PLATES

PLATE I

p. 2157

"*Hold up, you sluts,/Your aprons mountant.*"
(*IV.iii*)

From Vol. V of Nicholas Rowe's
edition of *The Works of Mr. William
Shakespear* (London, 1709).
Folger Shakespeare Library.

PLATE II

P. Fourdrinier sculp.   V. 6. p. 99.

Timon is visited by Alcibiades, Phrynia, and Timandra. (IV.iii)

From *The History of Timon of Athens, the Man-Hater. Altered by Mr. Shadwell.* (London, 1736). Folger Shakespeare Library. (Cf. Rowe edition, Plate I)

PLATE III

Timon with Alcibiades, Phrynia, and Timandra.
(IV.iii)

From Vol. V of Sir Thomas Han-
mer's edition of *The Works of
Shakespear* (Oxford, 1744). Folger
Shakespeare Library.

PLATE IV

Act IV. _Scene V._

———There's a Medlar for thee eat it.

Apemantus offers Timon a medlar. (IV.iii)

From an edition of *Timon* "as performed at the Theatre-Royal, Drury Lane" (London, 1773). Folger Shakespeare Library.

PLATE V

Timon without the gates of Athens.

From Boydell's *Shakespeare Gallery* (London, 1803). Folger Shakespeare Library.

PLATE VI

Vol. 2. *p. 191*

The Last Entertainment of Timon

Timon throws water in the faces of his friends.
(III.vi)

From Charles Lamb's account of
Timon in Vol. II of the *Tales From
Shakespear* (London, 1807). Folger
Shakespeare Library.

PLATE VII

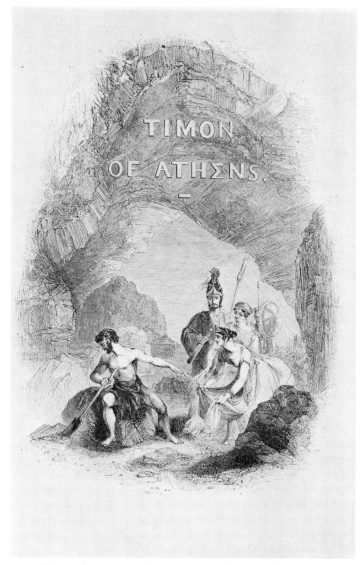

*"There's more gold: Do you damn others, and
let this damn you." (IV.iii)*

PLATE VIII

RE-ENTER·CVPID
ACT·I·SCENE·II

"*Re-enter Cupid, with a mask of Ladies as Ama-*
zons, with lutes in their hands, dancing and
playing." *(I.ii)*

Byam Shaw drawing for the Chiswick edition (London, 1902). Folger Shakespeare Library.

PLATE IX

"Grant I may never prove so fond,/ To trust
man on his oath or bond." (I.ii)

Byam Shaw drawing of Apemantus's
grace for the Chiswick edition
(London, 1902). Folger Shakespeare
Library.

PLATE X

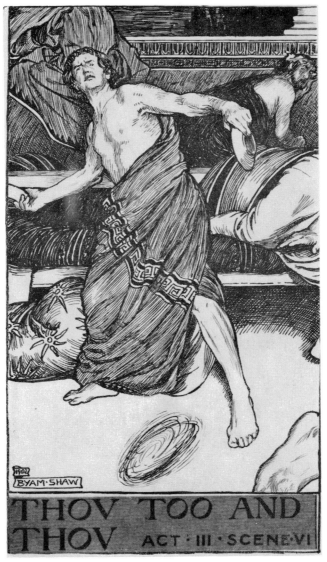

"Uncover, dogs, and lap!" *(III.vi) Timon hurls*
dishes at his false friends.

Byam Shaw drawing for the Chiswick edition of Shakespeare (London, 1902). Folger Shakespeare
Library.

PLATE XI

*Fortune and "all kind of natures . . . whose
eyes are on this sovereign lady fix'd." (I.i)*

Wyndam Lewis drawing for Max
Goschen's edition (London, 1912).
Folger Shakespeare Library.

PLATE XII

The fractionated world image depicted in Act II.

An illustration by Wyndam Lewis
for Max Goschen's edition of *Timon*
(London, 1912). Folger Shakespeare
Library.

PLATE XIII

*The entreaty of the Senators, Timon's negation
and death.*

Symbolic representation of Act V of
Timon by Wyndam Lewis for Max
Goschen's edition (London, 1912).
Folger Shakespeare Library.

PLATE XIV

Scene from the Timon of Athens *presentation at the Stratford, Ontario, Festival, Chichester Festival Theatre, Chichester, England, April, 1964.*

Part One

STRUCTURE

I

LORD TIMON'S FRAME: *The Early Editors*

A thing slipt idly from me. (I.i)

W ITH the exception of Romantic and mid-twentieth-century criticism, the literary criticism of Shakespeare's *Timon of Athens* has dealt primarily with the structure of the play. The structure has generally been considered to be poor. This judgment has been based on the assumption that the play should have a coherent development in the action from beginning to end and the conviction that this development did not occur. Either the lack of coherence has not been explained, or it has been attributed to corruption by the printers of the Folio of 1623, or to poor writing on Shakespeare's part.

The structural difficulties in *Timon* appear to have come to critical attention at least partially through the attempts of the early editors to divide the play into acts. The need to divide *Timon* into acts was the subject of what was, so far as I am aware, the first textual criticism of *Timon*. This criticism consisted of a sen-

tence in Gerard Langbaine's *An Account of the English
Dramatick Poets* (Oxford, 1691). Langbaine wrote,
"The Play is originally Shakespeare's; but so imperfectly
printed, that 'tis not divided into Acts."[1]

Timon, which was not divided into acts in the Folio
of 1623, was first so divided by Nicholas Rowe, first
editor of Shakespeare's plays (1709),[2] who divided into
five acts all of Shakespeare's tragedies. Roughly, these
divisions appear to follow certain junctures in normal
plot development. With the exception of the division
between Acts IV and V, the act divisions which Rowe
made for *Timon* have been accepted by succeeding
editors. When Rowe attempted to designate a fifth act
in *Timon*, he was confronted with a peculiar problem.
The fourth act of the play begins with Timon as an
exile in the woods near Athens and continues with a
long series of visits to Timon from various individuals—
Timon's Steward with two or three servants, Alcibiades
and two prostitutes, Apemantus, some bandits. Rowe
chose, apparently arbitrarily, to end the fourth act
after the visit of the bandits (IV.iii). Actually, the
visitors continue to arrive: the Steward reappears, followed by the Poet and Painter, and some Senators. Had
Rowe terminated Act IV at the end of this sequence of
visits (V.ii), Act V would have consisted of only 120
lines.

Because Rowe was a professional dramatist working
within one hundred years of Shakespeare's time, Rowe's
scene divisions are also of interest. They isolate in long
scenes balanced series of episodes. (These groups of
episodes have subsequently been emphasized by those
critics who see *Timon* as a morality-type play.)[3] Unity
of place, rather than unity of action, appears to have
dominated Rowe's thinking in determining the portions of the play to allot to each of the scenes in the five

acts, which consist of one, two, four, three, and two scenes respectively.

The entire first act consists of one scene which Rowe labels "A Hall in Timon's House." It depicts in unbroken sequence the foreshadowing of Timon's relationship to his false friends as well as the relationship itself as revealed by their petitions and flattery prior to and during the first banquet.

After the brief scene in which the Senator speaks of Timon's debts (II.i), Rowe puts the remainder of Act II in the one long scene, including the attempts of usurers to collect money from Timon, the discussion of these attempts by Apemantus and the Fool, the dialogue about Timon's debts which takes place between Timon and the Steward, and Timon's despatch of his servants to ask money of his false friends. Although Rowe labels this scene, "Timon's Hall," obviously the long dialogue between Apemantus and the Fool (II.ii) could not take place in Timon's Hall because Apemantus says to the Fool, "I will go with you to Lord Timon's." The dialogue was criticized by editors in the nineteenth century as an indication of divided authorship or of the unfinished state of the play.[4] It has also been defended—in the unlocalized form in which it appears in the Folio—as representational of a comparable sequence of events in real life.[5]

In Act III, under his own stage direction, "The City," Rowe groups in scene one a series of actions which appear to take place in succession at the home of Lucius, at a public place, and at the home of Sempronius. Later editors generally separated these scenes. Since, however, much of the action in this portion of the play is in the nature of sample reactions of Timon's debtors to the request for repayment, this material does not constitute a strong development in the action, but is, rather, cumulative evidence of a representational nature, paralleling the various petitions received by Timon in Act I, the series of demands from Timon's creditors in Act II, and the sequence of visits to Timon in the woods in Acts IV and V.

No editorial crux is involved in Rowe's decision to have Act IV open with Timon "Without the Walls of Athens," another of the scene locations which he adds to the play (IV.i); nor is there controversy about the position of Scene ii, in "Timon's House." From there on, however, considerable difference of editorial opinion has arisen as to the precise divisions of scenes and the position of the division between Acts IV and V. Although editors agree that Act IV, Scene iii begins with "Timon in the woods" (the first specific scene location given in the Folio printing), Rowe, according to his usual practice, includes the successive visits to Timon in one long scene in which Timon reacts to the appearance of Alcibiades, Apemantus, and the Thieves, respectively.

Capell and later editors have not followed Rowe in beginning Act V with the soliloquy of the Steward—where at least the point of view is directed briefly away from Timon's—but have preferred to make a scene division at this point. Their attempts to determine the proper division between Acts IV and V are as arbitrary and unsatisfactory as Rowe's. Naturally, critics with a preconceived idea that the play should have five coherent acts were disappointed with the unusually long *catastasis*, consisting of the visits to Timon in the woods, and the failure of this sequence of visits to lead naturally on an ascending dramatic scale into the brief *catastrophe*. Critics sought various explanations for the difficulty. These explanations will be discussed as they present themselves.

Rowe's procedure, then, of using as few scene divisions as possible by locating as large a segment of the action as possible in one place tends to emphasize a series of balances in the play outside the traditional plot structure. Since Rowe worked nearer Shakespeare's own time, Rowe's practice may be one key to Shakespeare's dramatic intention for the play.

That Pope based his act and scene divisions of Shakespeare's plays on the French system of a new scene for each new character is explained in his introductory volume to his edition of Shakespeare's *Works* (1725).[6] Pope announces that "The Plays not having been before so much as distinguished by *Acts* and *Scenes,* they are in this edition divided according as they play'd them. . . ." Pope attributes structural defects to a carelessly written "Prompter's Book" or to "Piece-meal Parts written out for the use of actors."[7]

Using this system—"as they play'd them"—Pope divides *Timon* into five acts of eight, five, seven, seven, and five scenes, respectively. Although Pope's act divisions correspond with Rowe's, his scene divisions are so frequent that each scene averages only 74 lines in length. The most startling result of this chopping process is Pope's decision to omit the brief visit of the Soldier to the woods (V.iii), which, if included on the basis of Pope's theory of scene divisions, would make a separate scene. Such an omission was bound to call attention to the structural condition of the play.

Theobald and Warburton, well aware of Pope's divisions, restore the omitted visit of the Soldier to the woods.[8] Hanmer follows Pope in omitting the Soldier's visit and inserting it in a footnote at the bottom of the page.[9] Apparently, Hanmer regards the passage as an insertion by an inferior writer, for in his general introduction to the *Works,* he explains, "Most of those passages are thrown to the bottom of the page and rejected as spurious, which were stigmatized in Mr. Pope's Edition."[10]

At about the time that Capell was attempting to find a more satisfactory act division for the play, Samuel Johnson's edition of Shakespeare's works was published.[11] Johnson followed Pope's scene divisions, but not slavishly. He made one less scene in Act I and one more in Act V. He clearly indicated that "in the original edition this play is not divided into separate acts, so that the present distribution is arbitrary, and may be changed if any convenience can be gained, or impropriety obviated by alteration."[12]

Johnson discovered difficulties in *Timon* in three places which have since been regarded as structural problems. Of the dialogue between Apemantus and the Fool (II.ii), Johnson suggests corruption:

> I suspect some scene to be lost in which the entrance of the fool, and the page that follows him, was prepared by some introductory dialogue. . . .[13]

Of the visit of the Poet and Painter to Timon in the woods (V.i), Johnson leaves open the possibility of bad writing:

> The poet and painter were within view when *Apemantus* parted from *Timon,* and might then have seen *Timon,* since *Apemantus,* standing by him, could see them: But the scenes of the *thieves* and the *steward* have passed before their arrival, and yet passed as the drama is now conducted, within their view. It might be suspected that some scenes are transposed, for all these difficulties would be removed by introducing the poet and painter first, and the thieves in this place. Yet I am afraid the scenes must keep their present order; for the painter alludes to the thieves, when he

says, *he likewise enriched poor straggling soldiers with great quantity.*[14]

Although Johnson includes as a separate fifth scene the passage about the Soldier in the woods (Globe.V.iii.1–11), which Pope chose to reject and include in fine type at the bottom of the page, Pope's attitude toward the passage naturally came to Johnson's attention, since Johnson was in the main following Pope's scene divisions. Johnson observes:

> There is something elaborately unskilful in the contrivance of sending a soldier, who cannot read, to take the epitaph in wax, only that it may close the play by being read with more solemnity in the last scene.[15]

Here, Johnson's suggestion is unmistakable that the difficulty with the scene may not be corruption but may be bad writing.

Whatever the reasons for the structure, Johnson's comments about all three of the above portions of the play point to what he believes are structural defects. Johnson's final statement about the structure of *Timon,* expressed in a footnote at the end of the play, is that "in the plan, there is not much art."[16]

Editors have preferred the act and scene divisions decided on by Edward Capell.[17] Capell notes that the plays are not divided into acts, that the entries are imperfect, and the exits often omitted.[18] These omissions Capell attempts to correct.

Capell divides *Timon* into five acts of two, two, six, three, and five scenes. Rather than following Rowe in beginning Act V with the soliloquy of the Steward (IV.iii), Capell delays the beginning of the act until the entrance of the Poet and Painter. Succeeding editors

have generally accepted Capell's divisions and Johnson's opinions.

Major efforts to determine act and scene divisions
ceased with Capell. The next editor, George Steevens,
was more interested in "regularizing" the lines in the
plays of Shakespeare.[19] Steeven's efforts stimulated
scholars into closer scrutiny of the condition of the texts
of the plays. In several plays which had "rough" lines,
the regularization later gave divided-authorship theorists the opportunity of equating the lines which
Steevens had found to be irregular with the work of
an "inferior" author.[20]

The irregularities of the Poet-Painter scene in Act
V, in which criticism of Shakespeare is only implied
by Johnson, are by Reed explicitly attributed to Shakespeare. Reed writes:

> I am afraid many of the difficulties which the
> commentators on our author have employed their
> abilities to remove, arise from the negligence of
> Shakespeare himself, who appears to have been less
> attentive to the connection of his scenes, than a less
> hasty writer may be supposed to have been. It is but
> justice to observe that the same regulation has al-
> ready been adopted by Mr. Capell.[21]

But Capell did not attribute his desire to change his
distribution of scenes (not limited to *Timon*) to Shakespeare's "negligence."

Johnson's criticism of the coherence of the Poet-
Painter scene and the defense of its structural coherence
by Ritson and Malone (to be discussed later)[22] were re-
corded in the Third Variorum of Shakespeare's plays
(1821).[23] With the exception of some critics in the Romantic period and in the mid-twentieth century, most
critics agreed with the comments which the Variorum
reprinted from Johnson—that "in the plan there is not

much art"—and attempted to find explanations for what they believed were deficiencies in the structure. Like a headache, their efforts have affected the entire body of criticism of the play.

FOOTNOTES

1. Gerard Langbaine, *An Account of the English Dramatick Poets* (Oxford, 1691), p. 451.
2. *The Works of Mr. William Shakespear*, ed. Nicholas Rowe (London, 1709), V.
3. A. S. Collins, *"Timon of Athens:* A Reconsideration," *RES* (April, 1946), XXII, 96–108.
4. See Chapters II, III, and IV.
5. Collins, *op. cit.*
6. *The Works of Shakespear*, ed. Alexander Pope (London, 1725), I, xviii.
7. Pope, *op. cit.*, p. xvii.
8. *The Works of William Shakespeare*, ed. Lewis Theobald (London, 1733), VI; and *The Works of Shakespear*, ed. William Warburton (London, 1747), VI.
9. *The Works of Shakespear*, ed. Sir Thomas Hanmer (Oxford, 1744), V, 76.
10. Hanmer, *op. cit.*, I.
11. *The Plays of William Shakespeare*, ed. Samuel Johnson (London, 1765).
12. *Ibid.*, VI.
13. *Ibid.*, p. 198.
14. *Ibid.*, p. 261.
15. *Ibid.*, pp. 271–272.
16. *Ibid.*, p. 276.
17. *Mr. William Shakespeare Comedies, Histories, and Tragedies*, ed. Edward Capell (London, 1768), VIII.
18. Capell, *op. cit.*, I, 4.
19. *The Plays of William Shakespeare*, eds. Samuel Johnson, George Steevens, and Isaac Reed (London, 1793), XI.
20. *The Pictorial Edition of the Works of Shakspere*, ed. Charles Knight (London, 1839), V, 338.
21. *The Plays of William Shakespeare*, eds. Samuel Johnson, George Steevens, and Isaac Reed (London, 1785), VIII, 464, or Boswell-Malone Variorum (London, 1821), XIII, 410.
22. See Chapter V for Ritson's and Malone's comments on this scene.
23. *The Plays and Poems of William Shakespeare*, eds. James Boswell and Edmond Malone (London, 1821), XIII. See especially XIII, 248, 252, 260, 298, 307, 316–318, 360, 375, 410.

II

MEAN EYES: *The Divided-Authorship Theory*

---

*To show Lord Timon that mean eyes have seen
the foot above the head.* (I.i)

WHEN Johnson questioned the coherence of certain portions of *Timon*, he obviously assumed that a play should have some interrelated or causal succession of events. Many editors and critics continued to assume that *Timon* should have this kind of structural coherence—a smooth causal sequence—and were disappointed when they could not find it.

Most editors agreed with Johnson that "in the plan, there is not much art." Some simply stated their disappointment with the interrelation of the parts of the play as dominated by the general character of the whole (the definition of structure as given in the Foreword). Many editors attempted to explain structural incoherencies. A few theorized that the ruptures in causal sequence developed from an awkward grafting of Shakespeare's *Timon* on the plot of an older play. A large number of critics saw the awkward junctures in the play as caused either by an uneasy collaboration between Shakespeare and an inferior dramatist, or by Shakespeare's having crudely sketched out a plot that was later filled in by another dramatist. Other critics argued that the play represents only a vigorous roughing out of a plot by Shakespeare, which, for some reason, he left unfinished—perhaps he realized he had made a poor choice of subjects for dramatic treatment or perhaps he had had a mental illness. Some critics— not many—thought that the structure of the play was good.

Critics who looked at *Timon* objectively were those who agreed with the Aristotelian concept of plot structure in tragedy which demands that the incidents in a plot should have an ordered interconnection or unity of action, so as to produce a plot with a beginning, a middle, and an end.[1] A hybrid approach to the play—partly objective and partly subjective—was adopted by critics who accepted the theory that the incidents in a play should have an ordered interconnection but whose thinking was tinged also with the Romantic idea that the entire creative work, including its structure, should be regarded as an extension of the author's mind. These classical-Romantic critics tended to find an inner coherence in the events in the play outside the formal plot development. Purely Romantic critics paid little attention to the structure of *Timon*. Their attitude appeared to be that the structure was Shakespeare's creation *ex se* and therefore good.

Those critics who held the classical point of view toward the play generally described it as breaking apart at the climax. In his *Essais Littéraires* (1828), Paul Duport finds that *Timon* begins on the true tragic note, but that in the second half of the play, the action falls apart:

> Mais là où la comédie s'élevait d'un degré, où Horace lui aurait permis l'accent tragique, lorsqu'il

s'agissait d'étaler les transports de colère d'une âme
noble qui vient de faire la triste expérience de
l'égoisme et de la perversité des hommes le poète s'est
oublié tout-a-fait; l'action qu'il invente est languis-
sante, décousue, bizarre.[2]

A similar attitude about the plot was shown more than
one hundred years later by Elmer Stoll. In *Art and
Artifice in Shakespeare* (1933), Stoll sees *Timon* as depending on a stock pattern, "artificial and outworn."
The plot is that of "love or generosity suddenly and
irrevocably turned to hatred."[3] Writing about thirty
years after Stoll, Peter Ure complains of the "static
quality" of the second half of the play.[4] Mark Van
Doren writes bluntly:

> If Aristotle was right when he called plot the soul
> of tragedy, "Timon of Athens" has no soul. . . . The
> play is two plays, casually joined at the middle; or
> rather two poems, two pictures, in swan white and
> raven black. The contrast is all.[5]

Duport's mention of Horace and Van Doren's mention of Aristotle suggest that these critics assume that
the play should meet traditional standards of plot development, that *Timon* should, in Aristotelian terms,
have a middle and that there is something wrong with
this middle part of the play.

If the structure is deficient by traditional standards,
editors who believed that *Timon* should meet such
standards were inevitably faced with a dichotomy, if
they also believed that the structure should be regarded
from the Romantic point of view as an extension of
Shakespeare's mind: they had to explain how a late
play from the mind of so able a dramatist could be so
episodic, so lacking in an ordered interconnection of
its parts. The obvious answer was that Shakespeare

was not wholly responsible for it. It was more than two hundred years after the publication of the play before an editor suggested that *Timon* "is not wholly the work of Shakspere." This possibility of divided authorship was made by Charles Knight in his edition of Shakespeare in 1839.[6]

Knight agreed with Johnson that the following scenes lack an ordered interconnection with the rest of the play: Apemantus and the Fool (II.ii.47–128); the visit of the Poet and Painter to Timon (V.i.1–119); and the visit of the Soldier to the woods (V.iii). Knight also was concerned about the structural coherence of the Alcibiades-Senate scene (III.v.1–119), the position of which, it will be seen, disturbed Shadwell.[7]

Studying these scenes closely, Knight decided that their style was not characteristic of Shakespeare. They contained jingling couplets and crude prose, the kind of writing which belonged to an earlier period in English literature. In each of the questionable scenes, Knight moved from structural criticism into a criticism of thought and style.

For instance, in the scene between Apemantus and the Fool, Knight first criticizes the structure:

> Johnson saw the want of connexion between this dialogue and what had preceded it. . . . We shall have occasion to notice this want of connexion in other scenes of the play.[8]

Knight then criticizes the thought and style. He finds poverty of thought and crudity of verse. Specifically:

> The whole thing wants the spirit of Shakspere, and it wants also the play upon words which he almost invariably employed on such occasions.[9]

Similarly, the Alcibiades-Senate scene has bad structure: "stands here strictly as an episode," and a prim-
itive style:

> The scene between Alcibiades and the Senate con-
> sists of about a hundred and twenty lines. Of these
> lines twenty-six form rhyming couplets. This of it-
> self is enough to make us look suspiciously upon the
> scene, when presented as the work of Shakspere.[10]

The scene appears "to belong to a drama of which the
story . . . formed a much more important feature than
in the present play." Knight also finds the Poet-Painter
scene in the fifth act unmetrical in a way characteristic
of the plays which preceded Shakespeare. Timon's
asides are in "unmetrical blank-verse, which reads like
prose, and jingling couplets which want the spirit of
poetry." The passage about the Soldier in the woods
is "marked by the same characteristics."[11]

Proceeding from structure to style, Knight has decided that certain portions of the play were not written
by Shakespeare. But he needs a surer way of determining the "Shaksperian" and "non-Shaksperian" parts of
the play, as well as those parts merely "touched-up" by
Shakespeare. He finds it in the previous attempt to
"regularize" the lines in Shakespeare's plays by George
Steevens, who had found it necessary to "regularize"
an unusual number of rough lines in *Timon*.[12] Comparing the passages in the play which he regards as
structurally incoherent with the portions of *Timon*
which Steevens found it necessary to "regularize,"
Knight arrives at the following conclusion:

> For it is a most remarkable fact that, in all those
> passages of which there cannot be a doubt that they
> were *wholly* written by our poet, there is no confusion
> of prose for verse.[13]

Needless to say, certain other passages had required regulation beyond those in the supposedly incoherent scenes, so that the process of determining "Shaksperian" and "non-Shaksperian" portions inevitably extended to include the entire play.

Knight believes that "Shakspere was satisfied to take the frame-work, as he found it" of "a play originally produced by an artist very inferior to Shakspere, and which probably retained possession of the stage for some time in its first form."[14]

Knight had skilfully laid the foundation for the theory of divided authorship of *Timon*. A succession of editors and critics adopted the theory, each varying somewhat from Knight in conjecturing how it occurred that Shakespeare wrote only part of the play and in deciding what parts of *Timon* were Shakespeare's. Some editors accepted Knight's suggestion that Shakespeare had grafted *Timon* on an older play while others saw *Timon* as a play which Shakespeare had sketched out and which had been completed by another dramatist.

Howard Staunton, who agreed with Knight that *Timon* was grafted on an older play, attempted to find the original play source.[15] Staunton studied *Timon* in relation to the old Timon play in manuscript, which had been edited by Alexander Dyce in 1842,[16] and concluded that "there is not the slightest reason for believing that Shakespeare ever saw it." Rather, Staunton decided, both plays have a common and an as yet unknown source. It is this "common source," which "recast and improved by Shakespeare, forms the play before us."[17]

Dyce himself did not believe that the academic comedy which he edited was the source of Shakespeare's play, but he was inclined to believe that Shakespeare had based *Timon* on an older play. In his first edition

of Shakespeare's plays, published in 1857, Dyce reprints
Johnson's criticism of the lack of coherence of certain
scenes in the play, but Dyce does not comment on the
possibility of a show-through, in Shakespeare's *Timon,*
of lines from an older play.[18] In his edition of 1866,
however, Dyce has inclined slightly toward acceptance
of Knight's theory that Shakespeare partially recast and
improved an older play.[19]

In his edition of Shakespeare's plays (1847), Gulian
Verplanck accepts Knight's theory of divided authorship but suggests a variety of assumptions on which it
might be based.[20] Perhaps Knight is correct in assuming that *Timon* is adapted from an older play. On the
other hand, *Timon's* "turbid obscurity" in parts may
indicate that it is descended from the satires of
Gascoigne, Marston, and Hall. Obscurity was a required characteristic of classical satire. The "other
dramatist" involved may not have worked on the play
prior to Shakespeare, but may have filled in a play of
which Shakespeare had made a rough draft, for although the play appears to have "unison of thought," it
contains certain parts written in a style uncharacteristic
of Shakespeare.

Rather than following Knight in using Steevens'
"regularization" as an index to the cruder portions of
the play produced by an earlier dramatist, Verplanck
looks for a contemporary of Shakespeare's whose style
agrees with that of the "inferior" dramatist. Verplanck
suggests—purely as a conjecture without going into detail—that Heywood might have been the second writer.

While not attempting, like Verplanck, to identify
the second author of *Timon,* Henry Norman Hudson
enlarges on Verplanck's suggestion that the play may be
Shakespeare's originally, but completed by another
dramatist. Such a dramatist might well be responsible

for the difficulties in the structural coherence of the play, such as the lack of interconnection with the rest of *Timon* of the scene between Apemantus and the Fool in Act II: "Dr. Johnson saw this gap. . . ." A like problem is presented by the episodic Alcibiades-Senate scene in Act III.[21]

Hudson goes beyond Verplanck in developing the divided-authorship theory, in that he gives a detailed listing of the "Shakespearean" portions of the play:

> I.i to the entrance of Apemantus; II.i and the latter half of II.ii, from the re-entrance of Timon and Flavius; IV.i and iii, except Flavius' first speech in IV.iii; V.i and ii. In the other portions of the play, there are some passages by Shakespeare, as I.i, after the entrance of Alcibiades; I.ii, immediately after Apemantus' grace; and in the last part of III.vi, the first half of IV.ii, and in V.v. Some portions of the play are of doubtful authorship, as the dialogue in I.i between the Poet, Apemantus, the Merchant, the Jeweler, and Timon, and parts of II.ii and III.iv.[22]

In his editions of 1851 and 1872, Hudson is content to list the above attributions to Shakespeare, but in his 1881 edition, Hudson has become more specific. He puts asterisks before each line of the play which he thinks was not written by Shakespeare.

To Hudson, divided authorship of *Timon* is theory. To Grant White, who acknowledges in his 1875 edition his indebtedness to Knight,[23] theory has become fact. In his 1883 edition of the *Works,* White states flatly that "Shakespeare wrote a large part, and all the more important parts, of *Timon;* but the rest, not inconsiderable in bulk, is the work of a very inferior artist."[24] White parcels out the scenes as follows:

> Act. I., Sc.1, is Shakespeare's until the entrance of Apemantus, with some touches from him perhaps in

the rest of the scene. Act II., Sc. 1, wholly Shakespeare's, and Sc.2 is his, except the passage in which
the Fool appears. Act III., Sc.1, the last part Shakespeare's, and he perhaps touched other scenes here and
there. Act IV. is wholly Shakespeare's, except the
latter part of Flavius's last speech, and Sc.5 is in
Shakespeare's grand style. Act V., Sc.1, is Shakespeare's after the entrance of Timon; Sc.4, Shakespeare's wholly. All the rest of the play is by another
dramatist, who was an unskilful worker and a dull
and clumsy fellow.[25]

White also is sure that the "dull and clumsy" writer
who completed the play is "of a younger generation."

Whereas no such positive deductions about the
authorship of the play appear in the Globe and Cambridge editions of Shakespeare's *Works,* the editors,
W. G. Clark and W. A. Wright, are not wholly un-
affected by the editorial opinions of their time.[26] In
the Globe edition, their primary concern is with emendations of words in the play, but in the Cambridge edition, they touch mildly on the question of authorship.
They reprint in full Dr. Johnson's criticism of the
structural coherence of the Poet-Painter scene in Act
V. Then, as with Knight, their suggestion of the possibility of divided authorship grows out of structural
criticism. The suggestion is made in connection with
the passage about the Soldier in the woods (V.iii), the
structural coherence of which, it may be recalled, Johnson doubted, and Knight had questioned. Clark and
Wright express the following opinion about the scene
(italics mine):

> The author may have changed his mind and for-
> gotten to obliterate *what was inconsistent with the
> sequel,* or the text may have been tampered with by
> some less accomplished playwright. Anyhow the close
> of the play bears marks of haste, or want of skill,

and the clumsy device of the wax *cannot have been invented and would scarcely be adopted by Shakespeare*.[27]

In this note, Clark and Wright give an illustration in capsule form of how structural criticism of the play has led directly into the theory of divided authorship. They make a categorical statement in the above note that Shakespeare could not have invented the wax incident. On what basis do they come to this conclusion?

Their argument appears to be that Shakespeare is universally acknowledged to be skillful, and that, therefore, if the incident is unskillful, Shakespeare could not have invented it. How is it that Johnson did not come to the same opinion? He found the same structural incoherence in the scene and "not much art" in the plan of the entire play. The answer seems to be that Johnson would consider it illogical to establish a causal relationship where there is nothing but association. Even if the evidence is objectively true, and the scene is unskillful, Clark and Wright have used specious reasoning in their categorical statement that Shakespeare could not have invented the wax incident.

With such eminent opinion supporting the divided-authorship theory, it is not surprising to find that H. A. Evans accepts as proved the theory that the play is only partly by Shakespeare. In his edition of *Timon* (1890), Evans writes (italics mine):

> No one now maintains that the whole play is the work of Shakespeare; that about half is his and that the other half is the composition of an inferior writer, *has been accepted as an established fact by all modern critics*.[28]

Like Evans, William J. Rolfe accepts the divided-authorship theory as proved. In his edition of *Timon*

(1895), he embellishes the theory by suggesting a reason
why the pagination of *Timon* does not fit the Folio:
the editors of the Folio were aware that the play was
only partially Shakespeare's and were reluctant to include it at all.[29] In Rolfe's criticism, however, there is
a sign that editors are beginning to worry that they
have overextended themselves in converting theory to
fact. Whereas in his 1895 edition of *Timon,* Rolfe
states flatly that *Timon* is "not wholly Shakespeare's,"
and prints the "non-Shakespearean" portions in small
type, he moderates his editorial policy considerably in
his 1906 edition. In the latter edition, Rolfe qualifies
his statement that the play is "not wholly Shakespeare's"
by writing that it is a theory to which the critics "almost
unanimously agree."[30]   He also prints the play in uni-
form type.

In his Temple edition of *Timon* (1899), Israel Gollancz accepts the divided-authorship assumption about
the play, but differs somewhat from Hudson and White
on the scenes which he ascribes to Shakespeare. Gollancz finds that *"Timon* contains a good deal of non-
Shakespearian alloy. The following pieces do not stand
the test":

> Act I.Sc.i. 189–end of the scene (?249–265;283–294);
> the whole of Sc.ii.; Act II.Sc.ii.45–124; Act III., except
> Sc.vi.98–115; Act IV.Sc.ii.30–50, (?) iii. 292–362, 399–
> 413, 454–543; Act V. (?) Sc.i.1–59;ii.;iii.[31]

Gollancz was one last major editor of *Timon* to support strongly the divided-authorship theory about the
play. Rolfe's 1906 edition, cited above, is indicative of
the tendency of editors to withdraw from a positive
statement on the question of authorship. K. Deighton
began the retreat in his Arden edition (1905). Here,

he maintains the position of "assigning to Shakespeare a very much larger proportion of the play as we now have it."[32] Like preceding editors, Deighton is concerned with the lack of interconnection between scenes, a difficulty "which Johnson was the first to point out." Deighton goes into the old problem of lack of coherence in the scene in which Apemantus sees the Poet and Painter approaching, and the visits of the thieves and the Steward intervene. Deighton is also concerned about the dramatic purpose of the "wholly unnecessary" scene of the Soldier in the woods. Johnson's suggestion may have merit—that some of the difficulty may be attributed to corruption by the players. Deighton defends the structural coherence of the Alcibiades-Senate scene—a scene not commented on by Johnson, but which Knight and some succeeding editors had questioned.

By Stanley Williams' edition of *Timon* (1919), the divided-authorship argument had made the circuit from theory to fact to theory. Williams is sure that Shakespeare wrote the main portions of *Timon:* "This belief in Shakespeare's priority has grown, and, unless some new subversive evidence appears, can hardly be shaken."[33]

Perhaps because editors made more thorough studies of the text, editors were quicker to reject the divided-authorship theory than were critics. (Some critics still hold the theory.)[34] At any rate, editors had become suspicious of the conflicting opinions of what constituted "Shakespearean" and "non-Shakespearean" portions of *Timon,* and after Williams, no major editor entertained the idea that the play was written by two or more authors.

Late nineteenth- and early twentieth-century critics paralleled the editors in their opinion of divided authorship. Dowden maintained in 1902 as he had in 1877 that other hands besides Shakespeare's were involved in writing the play, but that "those portions of the play in which Timon is the speaker can have come from no other hand than that of Shakspere."[35] In *Shakespearean Tragedy* (1904), A. C. Bradley asserted that Shakespeare is the principal author of *Timon:* "a weak, ill-constructed, and confused" play.[36] Writing of *Pericles* and *Timon,* Felix Schelling (1910) believed that "It is inconceivable that Shakespeare wrote all of these two dramas with their inequalities of diction, lack of accordance with a general design, and other striking defects."[37] As usual, we find the same pairing of the idea of divided authorship with the criticism of structural coherence.

The elaborate theories of divided authorship of *Timon* which were developed by the critics F. G. Fleay and E. H. Wright near the turn of the century will be discussed in the following chapter.

FOOTNOTES

1. Aristotle *Poetics* 7.
2. Paul Duport, *Essais Littéraires sur Shakspeare* (Paris, 1828), II, 284.
3. Elmer Edgar Stoll, *Art and Artifice in Shakespeare* (Cambridge, Eng., 1933), p. 3.
4. Peter Ure, *Shakespeare: The Problem Plays* (London, 1961), p. 46.
5. Mark Van Doren, *Shakespeare* (New York, 1939), p. 288.
6. *The Pictorial Edition of the Works of Shakspere,* ed. Charles Knight (London, 1839), V, 333.
7. See Chapter IX for Shadwell's treatment of this scene.
8. Knight, *op. cit.,* p. 335.
9. *Ibid.*
10. *Ibid.,* p. 336.
11. *Ibid.,* p. 338.
12. *The Plays of William Shakespeare,* eds. Samuel Johnson, George Steevens, and Isaac Reed (London, 1793), XI. For Steevens' concern with meter in *Timon,* see e.g., XI, fn., 566.

13. Knight, *op. cit.*, p. 334.
14. *Ibid.*, pp. 333, 336.
15. *The Plays of Shakespeare*, ed. Howard Staunton (London, 1859), II, 459.
16. *Timon*, ed. Alexander Dyce (London, 1842).
17. Staunton, *op. cit.*, p. 485.
18. *The Works of Shakespeare*, ed. Alexander Dyce (London, 1857), V, 275.
19. *The Works of William Shakespeare*, ed. Alexander Dyce (London, 1866), VI, 504.
20. *Shakespeare's Plays*, ed. Gulian C. Verplanck (New York, 1847), III, 3–7.
21. *The Works of Shakespeare*, ed. H. N. Hudson (Cambridge, Mass., 1851–1856), VIII, 9.
22. Hudson, *op. cit.*, p. 10; also, *The Works of Shakespeare*, ed. H. N. Hudson (Boston, 1872), VIII, 10.
23. *Mr. William Shakespeare's Comedies Histories Tragedies and Poems*, Riverside edition, ed. Richard Grant White (Cambridge, Mass., 1883), V, 319; *The Works of William Shakespeare*, ed. Richard Grant White (Boston, 1875), X, 201.
24. White, (1883), V, 310.
25. *Ibid.*
26. *The Works of William Shakespeare*, eds. William George Clark and William Aldis Wright (London, 1865), Note XVII, 315.
27. *Ibid.*
28. *The Henry Irving Shakespeare*, ed. H. A. Evans (New York, 1890), VII, 3.
29. *Timon of Athens*, ed. William J. Rolfe (New York, 1895), Preface and pp. 10–14.
30. *Timon of Athens*, ed. William J. Rolfe (New York, 1906), Preface.
31. *Timon of Athens*, *The Temple Shakespeare*, ed. Israel Gollancz (London, 1899), p. vi.
32. *Timon of Athens*, The Arden Shakespeare, ed. K. Deighton (London, 1905), p. xxi.
33. *The Life of Timon of Athens*, The Yale Shakespeare, ed. Stanley T. Williams (New Haven, 1919), Appendix C, p. 129.
34. See, for instance, Winifred M. T. Nowottny, "Acts IV and V of *Timon of Athens*," *SQ* (Autumn, 1959), X, No. 4, 497.
35. Edward Dowden, *Shakspere His Mind and Art* (New York and London, 1902), pp. 339–340.
36. A. C. Bradley, *Shakespearean Tragedy* (London, 1904), p. 245.
37. Felix Schelling, *Elizabethan Drama: 1558–1642* (New York, 1959), II, 31.

III

"TIMON" IN THE WOODS: *The Fragmentation of the Play*

The mouths, the tongues, the eyes, and hearts of men . . . /
Fell from their boughs, and left me open, bare/
For every storm that blows; (IV.iii)

USING Johnson's criticism as a starting point, Charles Knight had established a basis in structural incoherence for proposing a theory of divided authorship for *Timon*. Beginning with Knight's structural analysis or a similar one of their own devising, a few critics carried the matter of divided authorship to a *reductio ad absurdum*—and thus gave the play back to Shakespeare.

The first of these writers, Frederick Gard Fleay, believed that Shakespeare had intended quite a different plot development from the one in the existent *Timon*. "The play," Fleay writes, "is, in its present state, unique among Shakespeare's for its languid, wearisome want of action."[1] The explanation lies in interpolated, static scenes written by some other writer, "not one of which adds anything to the development of the plot." The "Shakespeare part," on the contrary, "never flags."[2] Since the "second writer" worked on an unfinished play of Shakespeare's, and Shakespeare wrote "the main plot," the "genuine parts" of the play show that Shakespeare intended a different division of acts from that which is traditionally made.

Fleay labels these hypothetical act divisions A, B, CD, E, and F. Whereas A and B would correspond with Acts I and II as established since Rowe, CD, or Act III would contain the central scenes by Shakespeare, or III.vi (part) and IV.i; E, or Act IV would contain, along with the material of the "inferior" writer, IV.iii (part), and V.i.57–118; and F, or Act V, would deal only with the death of Timon and the revenge of Alcibiades, or V.i.119–231, V.ii, and V.iv.[3] Fleay gives as "the chief reasons" for the usual division of Act V "the inordinate length" of IV.iii and the "extreme shortness" of Act V. Fleay supports this "specific analysis of the plot with regard to the bearing of each scene or portion of a scene on every other" with a "metrical analysis" of the lines in the play.[4] That is, he does exactly what Knight and preceding nineteenth-century editors did—he goes from an analysis of structure to an analysis of style, and uses the synthesis of these two studies to confirm his theory of divided authorship.[5]

On the basis of his "metrical tests," Fleay decides that Tourneur is the "inferior author." Fleay devotes about half his *Manual* to explaining these metrical tests. They consist of analyses of the percentages of prose, blank verse, irregular verse, and rhymes in Shakespeare's writing at various periods in his career and analyses of similar percentages in the writings of possible collaborators with Shakespeare. On the basis of these findings, an attempt is made to ascertain the probable authorship of any given passage or play in question. Fleay's assignment of portions of *Timon* to Tourneur, however, scarcely appears to be an application of these tests. The possibility of Tourneur's authorship seems to be based on a single observation made in connection with the first fifty lines of Act IV:

> The style of these, and especially the metre, is utterly unlike anything in the other plays of Shakespeare. It is marked by great irregularity, many passages refusing to be orthodox, even under torture; it abounds in rhymes, in emphatic and unemphatic passages alike; the rhymes are often preceded by incomplete lines; one of the rhyming lines is frequently imperfect or Alexandrine. This style was introduced by Webster, and followed by Tourneur, who are the chief masters therein. It has some considerable power in these authors' own class of subjects—the horrible—as in the *Dutchess of Malfy,* or *The Revenger's Tragedy,* but is utterly unsuitable here.[6]

Assigning part of *Timon* to Tourneur on the above evidence was sharply criticized by E. K. Chambers in 1924.[7] In his Annual Lecture to the British Academy, Chambers reproved Fleay not only for his treatment of *Timon* but for that of the other plays of Shakespeare. Fleay, according to Chambers, "betrayed an imperfect sense of responsibility, both in advancing destructive notions without an adequate support of argument, and in withholding the explanations and justifications."[8]

According to Chambers, "The mantle of Mr. Fleay has descended upon Mr. J. M. Robertson."[9] Desiring to show that *Timon* was written by Chapman and revised by Shakespeare, Robertson based his "proof" of the lack of structural coherence in the play on an offshoot of the old argument about the lack of sequence of the scenes: the lack of sequence of the numbers of talents mentioned in the various scenes. To Robertson's mind, the variations in the numbers of talents confirmed the *non sequitur* nature of the action, which, in turn, was a result of divided authorship:

> Putting the problem in terms of our hypothesis, we get this: that Chapman wrote the "five talents," "five and twenty (thousand)" and "fifty talents" passages; that the message to the senators demanding a thousand talents is introduced by Shakespeare; and that the "so many" passages are also his. . . . But on any view, we are left with the data of a first writer [Chapman] who knew what a talent stood for, and a second writer [Shakespeare] who was in doubt on the subject.[10]

The matter of the varying number of talents in *Timon* is important because it has been used by some more recent editors and critics to support the "unfinished" theory about the play. These inconsistent numbers of talents are a sequence of "five," "fifty," "so many," and "fifty five hundred" (I.i.99; II.ii.103; III.ii.13, 40, 42). Capell had put a hyphen between "fifty" and "five" in the Folio's "fifty five hundred Talents" (III.ii.42), but aside from this emendation, the sequence did not seem to disturb eighteenth-century editors before Steevens. Steevens suggested that the numbers of talents "were not expressly set down by Shakspere":

> If this was the case, the player who represented the character spoke of the first number that was uppermost in his mind; and the printer, who copied from the playhouse books, put down an indefinite for the definite sum, which remained unspecified.[11]

With reference to Steevens' criticism, Malone saw "no error" in the numbers of talents. For the phrase,

"so many talents" (III.ii.13), Malone found a parallel
in Lucullus' speech in *Julius Caesar:* "There is *so
much* that thou wilt kill me straight."[12]

Fleay believed that the phrases "so many" and "fifty
five hundred" talents "look like the work of a man who
had some misgivings as to his previous amount of 50
talents; but was finally too hurried to remember to
alter it."[13] Fleay states positively that Shakespeare drew
the mention of the "five" talents (I.i.99) from Lucian,
and that the "inferior" writer copied the larger sums
from Plutarch.[14]

A hint for the development of the "unfinished"
theory was contained in Grant White's comment about
"so many talents" (italics mine):

> Possibly used (like "so and so") for an indefinite
> notion; but also *probably the presence in the text of
> a mere memorandum left from the first draft.* It would
> hardly be used twice in the course of a few speeches.
> The sum mentioned by Lucullus is so enormously
> great that it is quite surely the result of some error.[15]

The use of the indefinite numbers of talents in the
play to support the "unfinished" theory about *Timon*
gained impetus when Robertson's argument—that
Shakespeare was confused about the value of the
talent—was taken over by Terence Spencer to show
that *Timon* is a "rough draft" by Shakespeare.[16] In op-
position to the opinion of K. Deighton, editor of the
Arden edition of 1905, H. J. Oliver, editor of the new
Arden edition of *Timon* (1959), uses Robertson's and
Spencer's presentation of the talent argument to show
that "the only possible explanation" for the condition
of the play is that it is a rough draft.[17] (Deighton had
expressed the opinion that "neither Shakespeare nor
the second author, supposing his presence, knew or

cared to remember the real value of a talent.")[18] But to Oliver, Robertson's argument "clinches the case for incompleteness."[19] As Chambers observed in connection with Fleay's and Robertson's work, "We approach the point where scholarship merges itself in romance."[20]

Chambers also wrote that Fleay's self-confidence "hypnotized" his successors. Among them was Ernest Hunter Wright, who wrote an entire book on the authorship of the play (1910), in which he added a new set of parts of the play written by Shakespeare and parts written by an "inferior" author. In the Preface, Wright pays homage to Fleay as follows (italics mine):

> The name of the late Mr. F. G. Fleay occurs at many points in succeeding pages where I have presumed to disagree with him; but I should not like to omit a statement that at many others I was fortunate in the opportunity to *follow in his lead, whether by adopting his conclusions or developing my own from his suggestions.*[21]

Like preceding exponents of divided authorship, Wright builds his arguments on an enlargement of the old Johnsonian criticism of structural coherence. He argues that Johnson recognized the structural inconsistencies in the play, but failed to realize that the difficulties were caused by dual authorship:

> Thus when Johnson saw a poet and a painter announced as on the point of entering in one scene but not actually arriving until three scenes later, he thought "it might be suspected that some scenes were transposed"; though he discovered that they could in no way be rearranged. And when he found a page and a fool chatting glibly of the letters they are bringing from their mistresses to Timon and to Alcibiades—said page and fool, however, never in the least divulging, who they or their mistresses may be, or what the

letters may contain—he imagined that some scene had
been lost which would have introduced them and explained their dialogue. "It is well known," says Johnson in a sentence that sums up his explanation of the
irregularities of the play, "that the players often
shorten speeches to quicken the representation; and
it may be suspected that they sometimes performed
their amputations with more haste than judgment."[22]

Wright agrees with Johnson that there are structural difficulties in the play:

> In one place a thread of plot is made to lead up
> carefully to a climactic scene—and then the scene is
> left out. In another, a strategic scene is put in with-
> out any thread of plot to lead up to it and explain
> it. The whole plot is therefore none too continuous.
> It begins, halts, starts again, skips, gets twisted, takes
> on new motives, and comes finally to a somewhat un-
> natural end.[23]

But rather than following Johnson in attributing
the interruptions in the sequence of scenes to corruption by the players or to careless transmission of the
manuscript, Wright sees the inconsistencies as caused
by dual authorship. Like the preceding divided-authorship theorists, Wright moves from a consideration of
structure to that of style, and uses the latter as a tool
to "prove" that two hands are involved in the writing
of the play. In some ten scenes or parts of scenes, the
writing is "too halting in expression, too tame and trite
in imagery," or "too lacking in dramatic fitness, in a
word, too uninspired, to pass unsuspected." In sum,
these scenes are "unworthy of Shakspere."[24]

The "unworthy" portions can be identified by their
many rhyming lines, quick shifts from prose to verse,
and irregular lines, the last consisting of lines of ten
syllables which are unscannable, those with twelve or

fourteen syllables, sometimes scannable and sometimes not, and those with six, seven, or eight syllables, scannable or not.

Wright gives two long tables of percentages of feminine endings, run-on lines, rhymes, and irregular lines of the "spurious" author and Shakespeare.[25] In preparing these tables, Wright lost sight of three facts. First, in deciding what to measure, he neglected to consider that anyone could observe the due proportion of mechanical details and still not write like Shakespeare. Second, in deciding how to measure, he failed to define adequately his criteria of measurement. For instance, how can he define a line as "irregular" when he himself admits "the impossibility of telling whether certain passages are meant for prose or verse"?[26] Third, his determination of the results of his statistical analysis is equally misleading. Finding that 50 per cent of ten lines selected as Shakespeare's in the first scene have feminine endings is like finding that 50 per cent of the married English students in a department flunk when there are two married students in a department of one hundred. Then, Wright compares percentages for Shakespeare and the "inferior" author based on varying quantities of material. For instance, in Act IV, he finds that in the material he attributes to Shakespeare in Scene iii—lines 1–291, 376–463, 479–508, and 530–543—there are 27 per cent of run-on lines and only 4 per cent of irregular lines, whereas in IV.iii.362–372—which he gives to the "spurious" author—there are only 8 per cent of run-on lines (one line) but 15 per cent of irregular lines (two lines).[27]

If other scholars had independently arrived at the same divisions of authorship between Shakespeare and the second author, the theory would have been more credible. But Fleay was equally sure of different ascrip-

tions. Wright attributes to Shakespeare I.i; II.i. ii. 1–46,
132–242; III.i.ii.vi; IV.i.ii.1–29, iii.1–291, 376–463,
479–508, 530–543; V.i.ii.iv. Fleay, on the other hand,
ascribes only certain passages of I.i to Shakespeare,
specifically 1–185, 249–264, 284–293. He gives III.i
and ii to the "inferior" writer, only lines 95–115 of III.vi
to Shakespeare, differs by ascribing to Shakespeare
IV.iii.363–398, 414–453, and V.i.57–231.[28]

Wright has a way of innocently invalidating his own
arguments, as he does with respect to this division of
ascriptions when he writes, "Hardly two authorities
agree entirely as to the passages each dramatist con-
tributed."[29]

Thomas Marc Parrott, who wrote a monograph on
The Problem of Timon of Athens (1923), agrees with
Robertson in seeing Chapman's hand in the play but
thinks that rather than revising a Chapman draft,
Shakespeare wrote the play and threw it aside, at which
time Chapman and a third writer revised it. Like the
preceding divided-authorship theorists, Parrott bases
his theory on structural considerations. Shakespeare
abandoned the play because of structural difficulties
inherent in the theme:

> To make a play out of this theme, it was necessary
> to invent a number of incidents, and weave them to-
> gether into a coherent plot leading up to the cli-
> max. . . . Invention was not Shakespeare's forte; he
> preferred to take his plots ready made. And the ab-
> sence of any true plot in the Timon theme involved
> him in arduous and perhaps unsatisfactory labour.[30]

Like the other divided-authorship theorists, Parrott
used stylistic tests to determine the parts of the manuscript written by Shakespeare or by another author,
Parrott's candidate being Chapman. Chapman's "char-

acteristic" style included weak openings to scenes, frequent use of masques, and formal debates. According to Parrott, these stylistic characteristics of Chapman are seen respectively in the Poet-Painter dialogue (I.i), which opens the play in a "moralizing" manner, also characteristic of Chapman; in the Masque (I.ii.129–170); and in the Alcibiades-Senate scene (III.v). Any material drawn from Lucian is probably Chapman's— "Chapman was far more likely than Shakespeare to use this classic."[31]

Parrott gives less of *Timon* to Chapman than does Robertson, who actually gives Shakespeare only one scene in the whole play: Timon's monologue at the beginning of Act IV.[32] One reason for the smaller ascriptions to Chapman is that Parrott disagrees with Robertson's attributing certain material to Chapman on the basis of verbal clews—the use of nouns as verbs, or the use of elipses, the omission of the nominative relative. Parrott argues that Shakespeare also used these mannerisms, and that they are, in fact, common Elizabethan idioms.[33]

A second reason for giving less to Chapman is that Parrott postulates the presence of a third writer. How Parrott came to add a third author to his variation of Robertson's theory is understandable. Parrott as a Chapman authority could not bear to have his idol labeled "inferior." Parrott's attitude is frequently seen in his paper, as in his discussion of V.iii, when he writes, "This scene is universally rejected. I cannot find it in my heart to saddle it on Chapman. It seems rather the work of the reviser. . . ."[34]

Parrott disagrees with Robertson on the significance of the large sums of talents mentioned in the play. Robertson, it will be recalled, saw the large amounts as displaying Shakespeare's ignorance of the value of a talent. Parrott points out that comparably large sums are mentioned in North's Antony—"which Shakespeare must have known almost by heart."[35] Parrott's defense of Shakespeare's use of these sums diminishes the force of Robertson's argument, which nevertheless, as already pointed out, was taken over by Oliver in the new Arden *Timon* (1959) to "clinch" the case for incompleteness.[36]

Parrott traces for *Timon* a "doctrine of continuous copy" very much like that of J. Dover Wilson which Chambers condemns in the article on "The Disintegration of Shakespeare" quoted above.[37] Shakespeare left the play unfinished because there is no development of situation in the original story. (Or, as Hardin Craig later expressed it, "There is no drama in mere non-participation.")[38] Parrott reminds the reader that even Shadwell had to "make" *Timon* into a play. After 1616, according to Parrott, Shakespeare's company offered Chapman the job of revising *Timon*. Chapman wrote the opening episode of the Poet and Painter and their later lines at the beginning of Act V, the banquet scene, the Alcibiades-Senate scene, the Steward's soliloquy at the close of IV.ii and his interview with Timon in IV.iii, "and with this returned the manuscript and drew his pay."[39] When the King's Men saw his work, they decided that Chapman's additions made the play too long. "Nearly all the Chapman scenes show signs of heavy cutting," which indicates that the manuscript was then "cut down, and patched up" by a third writer.

Even after all these vicissitudes, "Shakespeare's hand," Parrott assures us, "appears in every act."[40] His hand is particularly evident in I.i.95–151, 249–264, 284–293; II.i.ii.1–46, 132–242; III.i.1–51, ii.vi; IV.i.ii. 1–29, iii.1–239, 248–290, 371–454; V.i.119–231, ii.iv. Shakespeare's influence is dominant in the play's style because he wrote the original play.[41]

Not Shakespeare, but Middleton and Day are responsible for the original draft in the opinion of H. Dugdale Sykes who considered the "problem" of *Timon* in 1924, or a year after Parrott.[42] Sykes, that is, agrees with Robertson that Shakespeare revised an earlier draft but disagrees that this original version was by Chapman. Sykes believes that his hypothesis best explains such peculiarities as "the imperfect coordination of certain scenes." When Fleay and Wright split up the text, "allotting one scene, or part of a scene, to Shakespeare," they could not agree on the distribution because Shakespearean lines were sprinkled through both the Shakespearean and non-Shakespearean portions. The difficulty in making clear-cut divisions between the parts of the play by Shakespeare and those by the second author should have indicated to Fleay and Wright, according to Sykes, that Shakespeare touched up a play already written.

Now who could have written the old play? By serendipity, Sykes stumbles on John Day, who writes the same "short, snappy lines," and the same not very witty quibbles. Sykes proceeds to give parallel passages from *Timon* and Day's *Humour out of Breath* to establish "the indubitable marks of Day's hand in *Timon of Athens.*"[43] Furthermore, the lines which do not look like Day look like Middleton—contractions, for example, and abundance of rhyme, irregular verse lines, and aimless shifts from verse to prose: "All these are characteristics of Middleton at the time the play was written."[44] Also, Middleton "dwells much upon duns and debtors."[45]

To prove Middleton's authorship of portions of *Timon,* Sykes asks the reader to compare *Timon,* III.i.5–7: "I dreamt of a silver bason and ewer to-night," and Middleton's *Your Five Gallants,* IV.ii: "I dreamt

to-night, Jack, I should have a secret supply." Or,
Timon, III.i.8, "You are very respectively welcome,"
with Middleton's *Your Five Gallants,* II.i: "You are all
most respectively welcome."[46] Between them, Day and
Middleton are responsible for those same structurally
incoherent scenes which disturbed Johnson: that between Apemantus and the Fool (Day), the Poet and
Painter (Middleton), and the Soldier at Timon's tomb
(Day/Middleton). The scene between Alcibiades and
the Senate, another traditional textual crux, was written by Middleton.[47]

In deciding which came first, Shakespeare or the
"inferior" author, Sykes used the same technique used
by preceding critics. He examined the structure, considered it defective, devised a theory to explain it, and
used the style of the play as the argument to support
his theory. His attention to structure has been referred
to above. He rather naively revealed the reasoning
governing his stylistic tests—his desire to protect Shakespeare from the charge of bad writing—in the following comment:

> If we give to Shakespeare all the great poetry the
> play contains and all the good blank verse, and to the
> "unknown author" all the irregular, halting verse,
> jingling rime, and uninspired prose, it is clear that the
> division thus made cannot be very far wrong.[48]

At this rate, certain portions of most of Shakespeare's
plays could be ascribed to someone else. To quote
Chambers once more, "We approach the point where
scholarship merges itself in romance." Or at least,
where subjective material is involved, we approach
circular reasoning, since the critics are bound to have
made up their minds in advance to some extent, and
to slant their findings accordingly.

Although a few later critics, notably Tucker Brooke (1948),[49] Hardin Craig (1950),[50] and Winifred Nowottny (1959),[51] have casually expressed an adherence to it, or not ruled it out, the theory of divided authorship had burned itself up by the early 1930's through the energy generated by its overly ardent proponents. Now, the "unfinished" theory, suggested even earlier than divided authorship as an explanation for the textual state of *Timon*, began to spark critical attention.

ASCRIPTIONS OF ACTS AND SCENES IN DIVIDED AUTHORSHIP*

	SHAKESPEAREAN	NON-SHAKESPEAREAN
	Act I	
Knight (1839)............	i.	ii.
Hudson (1881)...........	i.1–185; 249–265; 284–293.	i.186–248; 266–283; ii.
White (1883)............	i.1–176.	i.177–293; ii.
Fleay (1878)............	i.1–185; 249–264; 284–293; ii.	i.186–248; 265–283.
Rolfe (1882, 1895, 1906)..	i.1–185; 249–264; 284–293.	i.186–248; 265–283; ii.
Gollancz (1896, 1899)....	i.1–188.	i.189–293; ii.
Wright (1910)...........	i.	ii.
Parrott (1923)...........	i.95–151; 249–264; 284–293.	i.1–94; 152–248; 265–283; ii.
Sykes (1924).............	No way of detecting Shakespeare's (slight) revisions of play by Middleton and Day.	
	Act II	
Knight..................	i.ii.1–46; 129–242.	ii.47–128.
Hudson.................	i.ii.1–46; 132–195; 204–242.	ii.47–131; 196–203.
White..................	i.ii.1–46; 132–242.	ii.47–131.
Fleay	i.ii.1–46; 132–194; 204–242.	ii.47–131; 195–203.

(Continued next page)

	SHAKESPEAREAN	NON-SHAKESPEAREAN
Rolfe	i.ii.1–46; 132–242.	ii.47–131.
Gollancz................	i.ii.1–46; 125–242.	ii.47–124.
Wright.................	i.ii.1–46; 132–242.	ii.47–131.
Parrott.................	i.ii.1–46; 132–242.	ii.47–131.
Sykes..................	*See* Act I above.	
	Act III	
Knight.................		i.–vi.(most)
Hudson................	vi.27–115.	i.–vi.26; vi.116–132.
White.................	i.31–56.	i.57–60; ii.iii.iv.v.vi.
Fleay	vi.95–115.	i.–vi.94; vi.116–132.
Rolfe	vi.95–115.	i.–vi.94; vi.116–132.
Gollancz...............	vi.98–115.	i.–vi.97; vi.116–132.
Wright.................	i.ii.vi.	iii.iv.v.
Parrott.................	i.1–51; ii.vi.	i.52–66; iii.iv.v.
Sykes..................	*See* Act I above.	
	Act IV	
Knight.................	i.iii.	ii.
Hudson................	i.ii.1–29; iii.1–465; 476–543.	ii.30–50; iii.466–475.
White.................	i.ii.iii.**	
Fleay	i.ii.1–28; iii.1–291; 363–398; 414–453.	ii.29–50; iii.292–362; 399–413; 454–543.
Rolfe	i.ii.1–28; iii.1–291; 363–398; 414–453.	ii.29–50; iii.292–362; 399–413; 454–543.
Gollancz...............	i.ii.1–29; iii.1–291; 363–398; 414–453.	ii.30–50; (?) iii.292–362; 399–413; 454–543.

	SHAKESPEAREAN	NON-SHAKESPEAREAN
Wright..................	i.ii.1–29; iii.1–291; 376–463; 479–508; 530–543.	ii.30–50; iii. 292–375; 464–478.
Parrott..................	i.ii.1–29; iii.1–239; 248–290; 371–454.	ii.30–50; iii. 240–247; 291–370; 455–543.
Sykes....................	See Act I above.	
	Act V	
Knight..................	i.120–231; ii.iv.	i.1–119; iii.
Hudson.................	i.ii.iv.	iii.
White...................	i.38–231; iv.	i.1–37; ii; iii.
Fleay	i.57–231; ii.iv.	i.1–56; iii.
Rolfe	i.57–231; ii.iv.	i.1–56; iii.
Gollancz................	i.60–231; iv.	(?) i.1–59; ii.iii.
Wright..................	i.ii.iv.	iii.
Parrott..................	i.119–231; ii.iv.	i.1–118; iii.
Sykes....................	See Act I above.	

* Globe numbering.
** Oddly enough, White claims that "Sc. 5 is in Shakespeare's grand style," but there are only three scenes in Act IV, in both the Globe and the Riverside editions. (The Riverside edition, which White edited, is based on the Globe.)

FOOTNOTES

1. Frederick Gard Fleay, *Shakespeare Manual* (London, 1878), p. 204.
2. *Ibid.*, p. 205.
3. *Ibid.*, pp. 197–204.
4. *Ibid.*, p. 197.
5. *Ibid.*, pp. 204–205.
6. *Ibid.*, p. 201.
7. E. K. Chambers, "The Disintegration of Shakespeare," Annual Shakespeare Lecture. *Proceedings, Br. Acad.* (London, 1924), XI, 92–93.
8. Chambers, *op. cit.*, p. 93.

9. *Ibid.*
10. J. M. Robertson, *Shakespeare and Chapman* (London, 1917), p. 134.
11. James Boswell and Edmond Malone, eds. *The Plays and Poems of William Shakespeare* [The Third Variorum]. (London, 1821), XIII, 318.
12. *The Plays and Poems of William Shakespeare,* ed. Edmond Malone (London, 1790), VIII, 54.
13. Fleay, *op. cit.,* p. 202.
14. *Ibid.*
15. *Mr. William Shakespeare's Comedies Histories Tragedies and Poems,* Riverside edition, ed. Richard Grant White (Cambridge, Mass., 1883), V, 343.
16. Terence Spencer, "Shakespeare Learns the Value of Money: The Dramatist at Work on *Timon of Athens,*" *Shakespeare Survey,* 6 (1953), 76.
17. *Timon of Athens,* Arden edition, ed. H. J. Oliver (London, 1959), p. xxvii.
18. *Timon of Athens,* The Arden Shakespeare, ed. K. Deighton (London, 1905), p. xiii.
19. Oliver, *op. cit.,* p. xxvii.
20. Chambers, *op. cit.,* p. 93.
21. Ernest Hunter Wright, *The Authorship of Timon of Athens* (New York, 1910), p. viii.
22. *Ibid.,* pp. 2–3.
23. *Ibid.,* p. 2.
24. *Ibid.,* p. 81.
25. *Ibid.,* p. 57.
26. *Ibid.,* p. 56.
27. *Ibid.,* p. 57.
28. *Ibid.,* pp. 55–56.
29. *Ibid.,* p. vii.
30. Thomas Marc Parrott, *The Problem of* Timon of Athens, Shakespeare Assn. Papers, No. 10 (London, 1923), pp. 27–28.
31. *Ibid.,* p. 10.
32. Robertson, *op. cit.,* p. 152.
33. Parrott, *op. cit.,* p. 14.
34. *Ibid.,* p. 19.
35. *Ibid.,* p. 12.
36. Oliver, *op. cit.,* p. xxvii.
37. Chambers, *op. cit.,* pp. 102–104; Parrott, *op. cit.,* pp. 30–32.
38. Hardin Craig, *An Interpretation of Shakespeare* (New York, 1948), p. 246.
39. Parrott, *op. cit.,* p. 32.
40. *Ibid.,* p. 20.

41. *Ibid.*, p. 19.
42. H. Dugdale Sykes, *Sidelights on Elizabethan Drama* (Oxford, 1924).
43. *Ibid.*, p. 19.
44. *Ibid.*, pp. 20–22.
45. *Ibid.*, pp. 23–24.
46. *Ibid.*, pp. 24–25.
47. *Ibid.*, pp. 37–40.
48. *Ibid.*, p. 3.
49. In *A Literary History of England*, ed. Albert C. Baugh (New York, 1948), p. 539.
50. *A History of English Literature*, ed. Hardin Craig (New York, 1950), p. 268.
51. Winifred M. T. Nowottny, "Acts IV and V of *Timon of Athens*," *SQ* (Autumn, 1959), X, No. 4, 497.

IV

"TIMON" IN CHAOS: *The "Unfinished" Theory*

. . . my long sickness/of health and living now
begins to mend,/and nothing brings me all things (V.i)

CRITICS who proposed the divided-authorship
theory as an explanation for the structural incoherencies in *Timon* were confronted with a
formidable demand for proof. To obtain this "proof,"
they disjointed the style of the play in order to show
two hands. Critics who proposed the "unfinished"
theory to explain structural difficulties were not required to furnish much proof. First, they were not
attempting to take the play away from Shakespeare,
to whom *Timon* had been given through its publication in the Folio of 1623; and second, they had only
to develop the traditional criticism of Shakespeare's
hasty writing;[1] that is, they had only to speed up the
metabolic process of his impatient creativity to the
point where he was not only too restive to correct minor
errors but even to complete the play.

Because the "unfinished" theory enables critics to
examine *Timon* not objectively as an imitation of life
but subjectively as an extension of Shakespeare's mind,
the theory has been particularly appealing to those who

prefer the Romantic approach to criticism. Like the divided-authorship idea, however, the "unfinished" explanation for *Timon* was triggered by the structural problems of the play and was supported by an analysis of the style.

The "unfinished" theory was proposed in 1815 by Hermann Ulrici, a critic of the Romantic school. He found the structural connections in *Timon* "occasionally defective," and the style "heavy"—"the turns are striking and sudden, while the abruptness and obscurity of the language are extreme":

> All these defects force me to conjecture that the piece may have wanted the author's last finishing touch, in consequence either of his retirement to Stratford, or his death.[2]

In 1839, Charles Knight, who promulgated the divided-authorship theory, considered Ulrici's observation and dismissed it on the grounds that *Timon* revealed two distinct styles of writing. To Knight's mind, the incoherencies in structure were produced by the confusion between these two styles rather than by the unpolished condition of one author's work.[3]

In the brief introductions to his editions of *Timon* of 1842 and 1853, J. Payne Collier mentioned the "apparent want of finish" in some portions of *Timon*.[4] His notes reveal that he was worried about the structural incoherence of the Poet-Painter scene in Act V. Collier commented as follows:

> *Enter Poet and Painter.* Johnson has truly remarked upon the inconvenience of commencing the fifth Act here, as the Poet and Painter were in sight of Apemantus before he quitted the scene. He suspected some Transposition of the scenes as they have

come down to us; but the difficulty is to arrange them
otherwise than as at present, and to begin Act V at
any other point.[5]

For almost one hundred years, however, succeeding
editors barely glanced at the "apparent want of finish"
of the play. In rejecting the "unfinished" theory as
untenable, Henry Norman Hudson, in his editions of
Timon of 1851, 1872, and 1881, wrote as follows:

> To this there are insuperable objections. For the
> parts in question are nowise in a sketchy state; the
> outline is generally filled up, but not with the Poet's
> genuine stuff; the fault lies not in a defect of execu-
> tion, such as it is, but rather in an uncharacteristic
> style of workmanship: in short, they are in no sort
> like an unfinished work of the same hand which
> finished the other parts, but show a totally different
> cast of thought, of diction, and imagery.[6]

To illustrate that the plot is "filled in" rather than "unfinished," Hudson cites the "filled-in" nature of the
"episodic" Alcibiades-Senate scene.

W. Wendlandt revived the "unfinished" theory in
1888, but his effort went almost unnoticed, as did E. K.
Chambers' first support of the theory in 1908.[7] In this
first supporting essay, one can think along with Chambers as he rather naively progresses from a consideration of structure, to style, to divided authorship (which
he rejects), to the idea that the play may be unfinished.
The theory was so unregarded that, in reviewing the various theories about the play in his book on *Timon*
(1910), Ernest Hunter Wright relegated mention of it to
a footnote. In this note, Wright observed that W. Wendlandt argued "feebly" that the play is wholly Shakespeare's, "though he thought that some of it may still
be in rough draft."[8]

It is well to pause over Wendlandt's neglected paper because it is perhaps the most acute analysis of *Timon* yet written. Wendlandt sees *Timon* as "a study" in which Shakespeare had for some reason not achieved a synthesis of the "inner" and "outer" form. Wendlandt defines the "outer" form as the structure as determined by the artistic demands of the early Jacobean period and whatever parts of the plot are taken over from the source material—in Lucian, Plutarch, or an early Timon play, such as that edited by Dyce. By the "inner" form, Wendlandt refers to the traditional picture of Timon as a misanthrope of a beastly nature and the nobler conception of the character developed by Shakespeare himself.[9]

Wendlandt believes that this fissure between outer and inner form goes deeper than *Timon* itself, that it reflects the dichotomy between the objective and subjective values in Jacobean life and heralds the victory of objectivity in the later Jacobean dramas. In a sense, Wendlandt approaches the play simultaneously from the classical and the Romantic point of view, and in merging this criticism in his estimate of the play, decides that in *Timon*, the breach between object and value is not reconciled.[10]

Yet Wendlandt believes that the play is one of Shakespeare's greatest productions, and that it is all written by Shakespeare. He builds his lengthy argument on the basis that both the form and the meaning of the play more closely resemble those in other plays of Shakespeare than they do those in the plays of any other dramatist.[11] Wendlandt's own summary reads as follows:

Das Resultat meiner Forschung ist dieses: dass die Kritik, da sie weder die Glaubwürdigkeit der Folio

I untergraben kann, noch die Aufführung des Timon
von Athen vor der Ausgabe dieser ersten Sammlung,
also auch keine Schauspielerrollen, nach denen das
Stück theilweise für den Druck zusammengestellt sein
könnte, anzunehmen berechtigt ist, noch den geistig
hervorragenden "Vorgänger," dessen Stück Shakespeare bearbeitet haben soll, überzeugend nachzu-
weisen, d.h. namhaft zu machen im Stande ist, noch
von einem späteren Redaktor vor der Folio I das
geringste Positive weiss, sich mit der Annahme
bescheiden muss, dass diese Tragödie, in Anbetracht
der ausseren, in der Ueberlieferung und der Aehnlich-
keit mit den Dramen der letzten Periode des Dichters,
sowie der inneren, in Idee der Komposition und
Gedankenfülle der Charakteristik liegenden Gründe
fur die durchgängige Autorschaft Shakespeare's . . .
und dass diese handschriftliche Kladde auf nicht mehr
zu ermittelnde Weise in den Bereich von Heminge
und Condell und als solche unverändert in die Folio-
Ausgabe von 1623 übergegangen ist.[12]

Scholarly acceptance of the "unfinished" theory of
Wendlandt and Ulrici followed the publication of an
outstanding paper and book by E. K. Chambers. In
the paper, which I have mentioned in connection with
the divided-authorship theorists, Chambers showed the
fallacies in thinking on which the divided-authorship
theories were based, not only the theories about *Timon*
but about the entire Shakespearean canon.[13] The paper
opened the way to a fresh consideration of *Timon* as a
work by Shakespeare. Chambers points the direction
for this fresh approach to *Timon* in *William Shakespeare: A Study of Facts and Problems* (1930). Here,
Chambers reviews the theories of the scholars who had
suggested a second hand in the writing of the play. He
finds that "none of the theories seems to me convincing
in detail, and their very multiplicity suggests that the
exponents are on the wrong tack." Chambers then
states his own view:

I do not doubt that it was left unfinished by Shakespeare, and I believe that the real solution to its 'problem,' indicated long ago by Ulrici and others, is that it is unfinished still. . . . Shakespeare seems to have worked chiefly on the beginning and end of the play, and to have left the middle acts in a very imperfect state.[14]

Having thus expressed his adherence to the "unfinished" theory about *Timon,* Chambers left the supporting details of the argument to be supplied by other scholars. In the New Temple edition of *Timon* (1934), M. R. Ridley does not add to these supporting details, but he is, at least, an early editor of *Timon* to admit the possibility that the play is "unfinished." Writes Ridley:

The more one studies the play the more one comes to feel that many passages are not so much 'corrupt' in the ordinary sense, as simply unfinished rough drafts that were to have been worked over. And if that is so, emendation is idle.[15]

In writing that if the play is "unfinished," its "emendation is idle," Ridley relates the theory of the play to a new editorial policy respecting it. Editors who believed that the play was by two or more hands regarded the play as such a hodgepodge that any emendations designed to clarify it were justifiable. Thus we find in the nineteenth-century editors from Knight through Gollancz an accumulation of earlier emendations and their own. But editors after Ridley who accepted the "unfinished" theory—particularly Oliver—desired to preserve the play in its "unfinished" condition, and were consequently chary of emendations. Alexander forecasts this trend in an article in *Shakespeare Survey* (1952).[16] Oliver's edition (1959) restores

an unprecedented number of the original Folio read-
ings.[17]

Chambers' statement of the "unfinished" theory
about *Timon* was quoted and enlarged upon by Miss
Una Ellis-Fermor. In a paper on *"Timon of Athens:
An Unfinished Play,"* in the *Review of English Studies*
(1942), she refers to Chambers' theory, and in accordance with it, analyzes *Timon* act by act. She proceeds
in the same way as did the divided-authorship theorists,
that is, she moves from a consideration of structure to
a consideration of style. She recognizes that *Timon*
reveals "inconsistencies in form and presentation" but
finds that the play contains "unassimilated prosodic
units" that are unmistakeably Shakespeare's.[18]

Like the divided-authorship theorists, Miss Ellis-
Fermor questions the coherence of the Apemantus-and-
the-Fool scene in Act II and the Alcibiades-Senate scene
in Act III. The former scene suggests that scenes or
passages "were never written or were lost." Act III
"gives an impression of being planned," but "there is
no consistent carrying through of the plan as in the
first and to some degree in the second." The Alcibiades-
Senate scene is a "strange and startling incursion." In
questions strikingly like those of Chambers before her,
Miss Ellis-Fermor asks the function of this scene:

> What is the trial that is in progress? For whom
> is Alcibiades pleading? What has happened? And
> when? What has it to do with what goes before? Or,
> as we are presently in a position to ask, with what
> follows? It tumbles suddenly into the action with
> the bewildering inconsequence of a dream. . . .[19]

Yet the scene is in the writing "clear and shapely" and
"Shakespearean in style." Miss Ellis-Fermor decides
that either it was part of a discarded subplot or the

supporting scenes were lost or never written: ". . . it has as it stands no connection with the preceding action of the play." If, however, a supporting scene earlier in the act has been lost or never written, "this scene, characteristically Shakespearean as it is in style, might in that case, have been functional, taking up its place in the action of the play:

> The relationship of Alcibiades to the rest of the play could thereupon become firm and coherent instead of disturbing us as it does by its inconclusiveness; the action of the final scenes of the play would take on a substance and a coherence that it badly lacks, and, in fact, the whole of Act V would be related to the main action.[20]

(Professor of Philosophy Ramona Cormier of Bowling Green has suggested the idea that the "friend" for whom Alcibiades was pleading might have been an inaccurate representation of Socrates. Such a possibility would lend balance and coherence to the theme of the injustice meted out to idealists.) In spite of the unevenness of the fifth act, it contains "mature writing." Miss Ellis-Fermor bases her version of the "unfinished" theory on "two great weaknesses in the structure." She believes that the action does not knit together Timon's fate and that of the people in the play, and that the character of Timon is inadequate to the theme. . . . "We miss the familiar Shakespearean relating of character to society." The latter criticism of the isolation of Timon will be taken up in connection with the meaning of the play.

Ridley had merely suggested that *Timon* might be "unfinished." George Lyman Kittredge was an early editor (1936) to argue the theory in any detail. He found the structure loose, the interlude of Apemantus and the Fool intrusive, and "real confusion as to

Timon's interview with the Poet and the Painter, and
his encounter with the Banditti":

> In IV, 3, 356, Apemantus tells Timon that a poet
> and a painter are in sight; but it is the Banditti who
> come up (399). Both Poet and Painter have vanished;
> they do not enter until the beginning of Act V.
> Such flaws and irregularities—as well as the de-
> fective interweaving of the two main strands of the
> plot, the Timon story and the Alcibiades story—are
> adequately explained by the obvious fact that Shake-
> speare never really finished the play. This theory is
> practically proved by Timon's epitaph (V.4, 70–73).
> It consists of two inconsistent couplets. Shakespeare
> found them both in North's Plutarch, where they are
> quite distinct; he copied them both and never decided
> which to keep. . . .
> The subject of Timon may have impressed itself
> on Shakespeare's mind when he was reading Plutarch
> with a view to his *Antony and Cleopatra*. Doubtless
> he worked on the play at different times, and, as we
> have seen, he never actually finished it.[21]

Arguing primarily, then, on the basis of *Timon*'s
structural irregularities, Kittredge is as positive that the
play is unfinished as he is that "There is nothing in
Timon that may not well be Shakespeare's own." Aside
from Ridley's timid suggestion that the text might be
unfinished, editors since Knight in 1839 had attributed
Timon to two or more authors. Kittredge's stand as an
editor of the play then initiates a fresh editorial approach to the text as an unfinished work. Kittredge
briefly dismisses one hundred years of scholarly research
and conclusions with, "Dual authorship has, as a matter of course, been suggested. . . . As for the second
author, critics are quite at variance."[22]

W. W. Greg's bibliographical studies of Shakespeare's plays confirmed Chambers' and Kittredge's

judgments that the play was unfinished. In *The Editorial Problem in Shakespeare* (1942), Greg was concerned mainly with stage directions, which he felt were "more directions for composition than production." For instance, "Enter Lord Timon, addressing himself courteously to every Suitor"; "Enter Varro's man, meeting others. All Timon's Creditors to wait for his coming out. Then enter."[23]

In *The Shakespeare First Folio* (1955), Greg enlarges on his view that the play is unfinished. The basis of his argument is the structural incoherence: "Indeed there is no clear link between the story of Timon and that of Alcibiades. . . . They might almost belong to different plays."[24] The play is not divided into acts or scenes; there is no record of its having been acted; and the play was a last-minute insertion in the space reserved for *Troilus and Cressida*. There is no doubt, in Greg's opinion, that *Timon* was printed from foul papers which had never been reduced to order. "It is all the more remarkable that the foul papers should have been at the disposal of the editors." Greg believes that Shadwell was justified in asserting that Shakespeare wrote *Timon*, but that he (Shadwell) "made it into a Play."[25]

The "unfinished" theory followed the divided-authorship theory not only in finding a basis in structural criticism, but also in beginning as "theory" and soon becoming "fact." In his prefatory note to J. C. Maxwell's edition of *Timon* (1957), J. Dover Wilson comments that "An unfinished Shakespearian play offers of course an almost unlimited field for speculation."[26]

In J. C. Maxwell's edition, the old argument of the incoherence of the scenes is again used to support the "unfinished" theory. Maxwell dusts off the same material used by the theorists of divided authorship but changes the terminology from incoherent "scenes" to "themes." Thus, the Alcibiades-Senate scene is "a vigorous roughing-out, of particular interest for the study of a theme taking shape under Shakespeare's hands."[27] He mentions that Una Ellis-Fermor shares his view (but she calls them "scenes"). Maxwell finds it impossible to put the "piecemeal treatment of themes" in *Timon* into a coherent picture. This roughness of execution is the radical criticism of the play. Yet "at a highly abstract level, it is easier to summarize without serious distortion than any of the plays."[28] There is unity of thought but not unity of plot.

Maxwell sums up his view of *Timon* by observing that "the sight of Shakespeare at the height of his powers struggling with material which even for him proves recalcitrant is more instructive than the successes of most dramatists."[29] That is, Maxwell subscribes to Una Ellis-Fermor's idea that the play is an interesting study of Shakespeare at work[30] (something to which E. K. Chambers did not agree as he considered the play atypical, and hence not necessarily indicative of Shakespeare's dramatic technique).[31]

H. J. Oliver agrees with Chambers that one should not infer too much from the play about Shakespeare's methods of composition.[32] In his introduction to the new Arden *Timon* (1959), Oliver quotes Chambers' and Una Ellis-Fermor's views to substantiate his own opinion that the play is unfinished. Oliver also uses as an argument for the unfinished condition of *Timon* an offshoot of the structural "proof"—the lack of sequence of the numbers of talents mentioned in the play. For this argument, Oliver uses J. M. Robertson's discussion of the talent, which Robertson used to support the idea that Chapman was the author of *Timon*. (Robertson's work is reviewed in Chapter III.)[33] Oliver believes that

Robertson's evidence of the inconsistent sums of talents mentioned in *Timon* "clinches the case for incompleteness."[34]

"Why then," Oliver asks, "did Shakespeare leave the play unfinished?"[35] His answer is that probably Shakespeare was influenced by dramatic difficulties inherent in the subject. This possibility—that the difficulty with the plot lay in a bad choice of subject matter—had been suggested by Romantic critics, by theorists of divided authorship, and by some critics who saw *Timon* as experimental. "No subject," Swinburne wrote, "could possibly be more unmanageable."[36] H. N. Hudson, a proponent of divided authorship of the play, had mentioned "the unfitness of the subject" for Shakespeare's purpose,[37] as does Hardin Craig, who also writes that the play "seems never to have been worked out in its complete proportions," but who does not rule out the possibility of divided authorship.[38] F. P. Wilson, in *Elizabethan and Jacobean,* considered the possibility that "The unfinished state of *Timon of Athens* may be a confession that he [Shakespeare] had blundered in choosing this theme for a tragedy."[39] Charles Sisson, whose ideas on *Timon* as a structural experiment will be taken up later, expressed the opinion that *Timon* was written "upon a theme and story which did not lend itself to perfection in form, but gave scope to much splendid writing."[40]

While some apologists for the structure of *Timon* suggested the above explanation—that Shakespeare had made a poor choice of subjects—other critics attributed the inconsistencies of the play to mental illness. In his *Introduction to the Literature of Europe* (1839), Henry Hallam conjectured that Shakespeare wrote *Timon* in a fit of depression.[41] E. K. Chambers thought it possible that Shakespeare dealt with *Timon* "under conditions of mental and perhaps physical stress, which led to a breakdown."[42] Tucker Brooks, who subscribes to the theory of divided authorship for the play, wrote in *A Literary History of England* (1948):

> Moreover, there is plausibility in Sir Edmund Chambers' suggestion that the completeness of the play might be due to a physical breakdown (not recorded), which could have cut short the poet's tragic period and put an end for evermore to these strenuous analyses of the human mind.[43]

Hardin Craig also relates the condition of the play to the condition of Shakespeare's mind: "There was disillusionment in the mind of Shakespeare when he wrote *King Lear*. It is just possible that it carried over into *Timon of Athens*."[44]

To summarize, many critics believed that Shakespeare had never completed *Timon*. Either he decided that he had made a poor choice of subjects or he had an unrecorded mental illness, which terminated, for the time being at least, his literary activity. Like the theory of the divided authorship of the play, the "unfinished" theory was an attempt to explain a structure which, by conventional standards requiring an ordered interconnection of scenes, was faulty. Very few critics found the structure of *Timon* to be good. Their views will be discussed in the next chapter.

FOOTNOTES

1. *The Plays of William Shakespeare,* ed. Samuel Johnson (London, 1765), I, xx.
2. Hermann Ulrici, *Shakespeare's Dramatic Art,* trans. by Alexander J. W. Morrison (London, 1846), p. 238.
3. *The Pictorial Edition of the Works of Shakspere,* ed. Charles Knight (London, 1839), V, 333.
4. *The Works of William Shakespeare,* ed. J. Payne Collier (London, 1842), VI, 501; *The Works of Shakespeare,* ed. J. Payne Collier (New York, 1853), p. xcviii.

5. Collier (1842), *op. cit.*, VI, 574.

6. *The Works of Shakespeare,* ed. H. N. Hudson (Cambridge, Mass., 1855), VIII, 8; *The Works of Shakespeare,* ed. H. N. Hudson (Boston, 1872), VIII, 7; *The Complete Works of William Shakespeare,* Harvard edition, ed. H. N. Hudson (Boston, 1881), XV, 184–185.

7. Wilhelm Wendlandt, "Shakespeare's *Timon von Athen,*" *Shakespeare Jahrbuch,* XXIII (1888), 107–192; E. K. Chambers, *Shakespeare: A Survey* (London, 1948), p. 273 [reprint of introductory essay from the Red Letter Shakespeare, 1908].

8. Ernest Hunter Wright, *The Authorship of Timon of Athens* (New York, 1910), p. 5.

9. Wendlandt, *op. cit.*, p. 137.

10. For the relationship between object and value in literature, see Robert Langbaum, *The Poetry of Experience* (London, 1957), pp. 12–17, 26.

11. Wendlandt, *op. cit.*, p. 127.

12. *Ibid.*, p. 109.

13. E. K. Chambers, "The Disintegration of Shakespeare," Annual Shakespeare Lecture. *Proceedings, Br. Acad.* (London, 1924), XI, 91.

14. E. K. Chambers, *William Shakespeare: A Study of Facts and Problems* (Oxford, 1930), p. 482.

15. *Timon of Athens,* The New Temple Shakespeare, ed. M. R. Ridley (London, 1934), p. 111.

16. Peter Alexander, "Restoring Shakespeare: The Modern Editor's Task," *Shakespeare Survey,* 5 (1952), 8.

17. H. J. Oliver, "Review of *Timon of Athens,* ed. by J. C. Maxwell," *SQ* (1958), IX, 407.

18. Una Ellis-Fermor, "*Timon of Athens:* An Unfinished Play," *RES* (July, 1942), XVIII, 270–283.

19. *Ibid.*, p. 278.

20. *Ibid.*, pp. 278–279.

21. *The Complete Works of Shakespeare,* ed. George Lyman Kittredge (New York, 1936), pp. 1045–1046.

22. *Ibid.*, p. 1046.

23. W. W. Greg, *The Editorial Problem in Shakespeare* (Oxford, 1942), p. 149.

24. W. W. Greg, *The Shakespeare First Folio* (Oxford, 1955), p. 409.

25. Greg, *op. cit.*, p. 411.

26. *The Life of Timon of Athens,* ed. J. C. Maxwell (Cambridge, 1957), p. vii. See also, *Timon of Athens,* ed. Maurice Charney (New York, 1965), xxii–xxiii.

27. *Ibid.*, p. xl.

28. *Ibid.*, p. xli.

29. *Ibid.*, p. xlii.

30. Ellis-Fermor, *op. cit.*, p. 271.

31. Chambers (Oxford, 1930), *op. cit.*, p. 483.

32. *Timon of Athens,* Arden edition, ed. H. J. Oliver (London, 1959), p. xxviii.

33. J. M. Robertson, *Shakespeare and Chapman* (London, 1917), pp. 123–134.

34. Oliver, *op. cit.*, p. xxvii.

35. *Ibid.*, p. li.

36. Algernon Charles Swinburne, *A Study of Shakespeare* (New York, 1880), p. 213.

37. Hudson (Boston and Cambridge, 1855), *op. cit.*, VIII, 8.

38. *A History of English Literature,* ed. Hardin Craig (New York, 1950), p. 268.

39. F. P. Wilson, *Elizabethan and Jacobean* (Oxford, 1946), p. 117.

40. *William Shakespeare: The Complete Works,* ed. Charles Jasper Sisson (London, 1954), p. 910.

41. Henry Hallam, *Introduction to the Literature of Europe* (London, 1837), II, 567–568.

42. Chambers (Oxford, 1930), *op. cit.*, p. 482.

43. *A Literary History of England,* ed. Albert C. Baugh (New York, 1948), p. 539.

44. Hardin Craig, *An Interpretation of Shakespeare* (New York, 1948), p. 248.

V

ON FORTUNE'S HILL: Timon *and Defenders of Its Structure*

*O, what a precious comfort 'tis, to have so many,
like brothers, commanding one another's fortunes!* (I.ii)

WHEREAS the majority of editors and critics of *Timon of Athens* considered the play to be structurally incoherent, a few thought the structure to be good, or at least, acceptable. These defenders were not limited to one critical school, but included the "classical" critics—those who ascribed to the Aristotelian doctrine that scenes should have causal interrelation to give the plot "unity of action"; the Romantic critics, who saw the play, including the plot, as an organic extension from Shakespeare's mind; and those who regarded *Timon* as an experimental form.

Of the three groups, the smallest consists of those critics who judged the structure objectively by classical standards, and found it good. With the loosening of the demands for form through structural continuity and with an increased emphasis on meaning, a somewhat larger group of Romantic critics was satisfied with the structure of *Timon*. But the largest group of critics to express contentment with the structure consists of the critics who regard *Timon* as an experimental play. These critics are interested in the form of the play only as a tool to convey the meaning. Their views form a broad base to the pyramid of pro-*Timon* structural criticism, the narrow peak of which is the classical criticism of structure.

Since he is generally regarded as a classicist, it is surprising to find that in his structural criticism of *Timon*, Charles Gildon is much more lenient than are many critics of the play. The leniency of this classicist toward the structure proves nothing, perhaps, except the subjective nature of criticism. Almost any critic can use almost any standards of criticism as helpful tools to approve or disapprove of a work of art.

In his "Remarks on the Plays of Shakespear," prefixed to Rowe's edition of Shakespeare's *Works* (1710), Gildon writes of Timon:

> It is plain that the Plot is not regular as to Time, or Place, but the Action may be look'd on as pretty uniform, unless we wou'd make the Banishment, and the Return of *Alcibiades* an under Plot, which yet seems to be born of the main Design.[1]

Gildon's finding that the Alcibiades incident is "born of the main Design" is of particular interest because, as indicated in the preceding chapters, the Alcibiades scene has been regarded by many critics as "episodic," and has been used as a strong argument for the divided-authorship and "unfinished" theories.[2] Gildon has reconciled one Aristotelian dictum—that "Of all plots and actions the episodic are the worst"—with another—that if what happens has causal interrelation, the plot has unity of action.

Support for the unity of action in another key scene

in *Timon* is furnished by three late eighteenth-century critics, Joseph Ritson, John Monck Mason, and Edmond Malone. The scene in question is the Poet-Painter scene (V.i.1–120), the coherence of which was doubted by Samuel Johnson. Johnson, it may be recalled, observed that the Poet and Painter are within sight (IV.iii.365) when Timon is with Apemantus, but that the scenes of the Bandetti and the Steward intervene before the Poet and Painter finally arrive.[3]

Malone defends the structure of the play at this point by minimizing the importance of coherence here:

> I perceive no difficulty. . . . Shakspeare was not very attentive to these minute particulars; and if *he* and the *audience* knew of the several persons who had partaken of Timon's wealth, he would not scruple to impart this knowledge to persons who perhaps had not yet an opportunity of acquiring it.[4]

Ritson and Mason argue the structural continuity of this same scene by resorting to the odd expedient of looking at the action not objectively through the eyes of the viewer or audience but subjectively through the eyes of the Poet and Painter. Ritson writes:

> If we allow the Poet and Painter to see Apemantus, it may be conjectured that they did not think his presence necessary at their interview with Timon, and had therefore returned back into the city.[5]

Mason is the most positive in his defense of the structural coherence of this difficult scene:

> Johnson's remarks on the impropriety of this scene are not well founded. The Poet and Painter were in view when Apemantus parted from Timon, and might then have seen him; but we may suppose that they

had no desire to converse with him, until after they had heard that he was possessed of money, and had enriched other people. The Painter's first speech seems to intimate that he had seen him before.[6]

Whereas these adherents to traditional standards of structure took an objective interest in the continuity of particular scenes, critics during the Romantic period tended to be interested in the structural cohesiveness of the whole play as a product of Shakespeare's creative genius. Romantic critics held a variety of attitudes toward the structure. As indicated in the preceding chapter, some Romantic critics (Ulrici, Swinburne) found the structure defective. Singer, whose interest in the meaning of the play will be discussed in the next chapter, ignored the structure. Notable among the defenders of the structure were Schlegel and Hazlitt.

Even Romantic critics like Schlegel and Hazlitt, however, who praised the structure of *Timon*, were primarily interested in the meaning of the play. Characteristic of their usual approach to works of literature— that of regarding the work as an organic extension of the author's mind—these critics looked on *Timon* in relation to Shakespeare's supposed mental and emotional condition at the time he wrote *Timon* and particularly his purpose—the meaning he hoped to convey. Structure was of secondary importance, to be mentioned somewhat briefly in terms of its usefulness as a vehicle for meaning.

William Schlegel was the first of the eminent critics of the Romantic period to praise the structure of *Timon*. Like Gildon, who defended the structural coherence of the Alcibiades-Senate scene (III.v), on the grounds that it was "born of the main Design," Schlegel defends the coherence of the same scene for essentially the same reason. He finds that the ingratitude shown by the Senate to Alcibiades reflects that shown by Timon's friends to Timon. Of the structure of the play, Schlegel writes:

> The story is very simply treated, and is definitely divided into large masses: in the first act the joyous life of Timon, his noble and hospitable extravagance, and around him the throng of suitors of every description; in the second and third acts, his embarrassment, and the trial which he is thereby reduced to make of his supposed friends, who all desert him in the hour of need; in the fourth and fifth acts, Timon's flight to the woods, his misanthropical melancholy, and his death. The only thing which may be called an episode is the banishment of Alcibiades, and his return by force of arms. However, they are both examples of ingratitude, the one of a state towards its defender, and the other of private friends to their benefactor.[7]

Schlegel, using the Romantic, subjective approach to the structural problem of the play, and Gildon, using the classical, objective approach, come to precisely the same conclusion about the structure: that the play has unity of action, and that the incident about Alcibiades, somewhat disturbing at first glance, is actually absorbed in the plan.

Like Schlegel, William Hazlitt is convinced that *Timon* has structural unity. In his *Characters of Shakespeare's Plays* (1817), Hazlitt looks at *Timon* through the eyes of Shakespeare and finds that the play "is one of the few in which he seems to be in earnest throughout, never to trifle nor go out of his way. He does not relax in his efforts, nor lose sight of the unity of his design."[8] Showing no interest in the coherence or incoherence of specific scenes, Hazlitt is deeply interested in the overall emotional coherence of the play as an ex-

pression of Shakespeare's feelings: Shakespeare is "in
earnest throughout" and therefore, the play necessarily
has "unity of design."

The relaxation of attention to the details of structure which is seen in the Romantic criticism of *Timon*
heralded an even more complete disinterest in structure
among the critics who see *Timon* as an experimental
form. In fact, for some of the "experimental" critics,
the indifference to structure approaches total apathy,
for they argue that structural unity is not essential to
the play.

Among the critics who see the structure of *Timon*
as experimental are Una Ellis-Fermor (who is primarily
a subscriber to the "unfinished" theory), A. S. Collins,
Charles Sisson, Peter Alexander, H. J. Oliver (who also
sees the play as "unfinished"), and E. A. J. Honigmann.
Miss Ellis-Fermor sees the structure of *Timon* as "revolutionary."[9] She relates it to the "full measure of the
structural freedom" of Jacobean drama between 1603
and 1613. The "revolutionary" change in structure appears to consist of the "non-realistic opening"—the al-
legory of Timon on Fortune's hill—and the amplification of the opening in the play itself. The opening
"serves its poetic purpose directly and economically" by
abandoning verisimilitude altogether: "The first scene
is partly occupied by a brief prophetic survey in semi-
symbolic form that balances the situation rather than
sets the mood."[10]

Ironically—because of Johnson's influential comment attacking the "plan" of *Timon*—A. S. Collins uses
a comment of Johnson's as a basis for defending the irregular plan of the play. In a paper in the *Review of
English Studies* (1946), Collins develops the thesis that
Timon is an example of Johnson's comment about
Shakespeare: that "What he does best, he soon ceases
to do."[11] Collins observes that "if *Timon* is the most

striking of his experiments, it is by that all the more surely Shakespeare's, a bold departure typical of him and not of any other. Could any play more clearly declare its deliberate intention to be different?"[12]

Two scenes regarded as non-Shakespearean by divided-authorship theorists for almost one hundred years—that of the Three Strangers (III.ii) and that of Alcibiades and the Senate (III.v)—are chosen by Collins as "two master keys" to an understanding of the structure as a sophisticated art form developed by Shakespeare from the morality play "only so much altered as to bring it very near perfection."[13]

The scene between the Three Strangers is a key to the intellectual content of the play and the Alcibiades-Senate scene is a key to the emotional content. The unity of the play lies in the simultaneous impact of the intellectual and emotional elements. The fourth act reviews the ground covered in the first three acts. Collins agrees that the announcement that the Poet and Painter are at hand (IV.iii.355) is misplaced, but "apart from such details," the fourth act is "very effectively handled."[14] When Alcibiades re-enters the play in Act IV, Scene iii, it is "to make ready for the play's ending, not by mere plot or action to bring down the curtain, but in a final lesson to restore sanity and human decency." The brief scene of the Soldier at Timon's tomb does look like "journey-work," but when Alcibiades appears, there is "nothing amiss," and "The play ends with an admirable brevity."[15]

Perhaps the above excerpts are sufficient to indicate Collins' indifference to the traditional habit of judging the merits of the structure of the play by its coherence in consecutive acts. To write of "*mere* plot or action," as did Collins, is indeed an innovation in structural criticism.

In his 1954 edition of Shakespeare's *Works,* Charles

Sisson concedes that the traditional structural criticism
of *Timon* is justifiable.[16] The structure is "loose"; the
interlude between Apemantus and the Poet seems out
of place; the Alcibiades subplot seems not well inte-
grated; when the Poet and Painter are announced, the
bandits appear instead; the two epitaphs at the end of
the play suggest indecision. Nevertheless, Sisson regards *Timon* as a "finished" play written on a theme
which did not lend itself to perfection in form. In an
introductory essay to Sisson's edition, Harold Jenkins
suggests that Shakespeare was following a current trend
among playwrights—that of displaying more independ-
ence from demands of formal structure: "The plays
acted by the King's men at this time reveal a drama
capable of bold experiment. . . ."[17] As examples,
Jenkins cites *Measure for Measure, The Malcontent,*
and *Volpone.*

Harold S. Wilson, Peter Alexander, and E. A. J.
Honigmann have noticed structural and other peculiarities in *Troilus and Cressida,* and Honigmann has suggested that both *Timon* and *Troilus* may have been
commissioned for performance at an Inn of Court.[18]
This hypothesis is used to explain the structural irregularities as being part of a special form for a special
group. In his paper on *Timon* in *Shakespeare Quarterly*
(1961), E. A. J. Honigmann summarizes these structural
comparisons with *Troilus and Cressida.* The plays are
comparable in depending on parallelism and analysis
for dramatic form rather than on suspense built
through cause and effect:

> Not only in the characterization of subsidiaries,
> but in Timon's long denunciations, in the essentially
> detached "putting of the case" by Alcibiades in III.v,
> in the chit-chat of poet and painter, even in the con-
> trived contrast of Timon's earlier and later speeches,

Shakespeare seems to assume his audience's penchant for abstraction and generalization.[19]

Timon's "sex-disgust" parallels that in *Troilus*—and "Inn of Court literature dwells with enormous relish on every sort of unchastity." The shock tactics of the sex theme are "not so much a personal obsession as a necessary ingredient" in a play for the termers. Also, both *Timon* and *Troilus* have inconclusive endings "for the sake of intellectual outrageousness." A special audience might prefer disturbing questions to resolutions: "Thus Timon's suicide is hinted at but not definitely asserted, the reformation of Athens proposed but not demonstrated."[20]

The very inconsistencies which convinced the proponents of divided authorship that Shakespeare wrote only part of the play were Honigmann's major proof that Shakespeare was the sole author. Such loose ends were an "unavoidable secondary manifestation of his genius." For this reason, "it cannot be sufficiently emphasized that though *Timon* is riddled with inconsistencies and loose ends, this does not set it apart from Shakespeare's other works but rather confirms its authenticity."[21]

Among the inconsistencies in *Timon* are the inconsistent spellings of proper names. These spellings were used by Fleay to confirm his theory of divided authorship, by Greg to indicate certain irregularities in Shakespeare's spelling, and by Philip Williams, H. J. Oliver, and E. A. J. Honigmann to suggest "two hands" in the transmission of the manuscript. Thus, Fleay writes:

> Phrynia and Timandra are called Phryni*ce* and Timand*ylo*. This is one among several instances, tending to show that the second writer worked on a badly-written MS. of Shakespeare's portion. . . .

> Ventidius in I.i, and II.ii, is spelled Ventidius or
> Ventiddius; in II.i, and III.iii, Ventigius or Ven-
> tidgius. I think this points to the same conclu-
> sion. . . . The editors, against all metre, but deter-
> mined to perform the impossible feat of making the
> play, as it stands, self-consistent, alter Flavius to
> Flaminius. I feel sure that the third servant in III.iii,
> was originally meant to be Flavius. The stage direc-
> tion in II.ii, is "Enter 3 servants." I fancy the original
> reading was "Within there! Flavius, Servilius, Fla-
> minius!" but after the second writer had altered the
> Steward into Flavius, he struck out the name in III.iii,
> and meant to do so in II.ii, but, in his hurry, struck
> out the wrong name.[22]

Disagreeing with Fleay that two writers produced the variant spellings, Greg sees the inconsistencies as an indication of uncertainties in Shakespeare's own spelling and of the possibility that *Timon* was printed from foul papers which had never been reduced to order.[23] Greg assumes that in a polished manuscript, such inconsistencies would have been corrected.

If the theory of Philip Williams is established—that "two hands" are indeed involved in the manuscript of *Timon,* but the hands are those of a scribe and one or more compositors—then the chair is neatly pulled out from under the theorists of divided authorship. Writing in *Studies in Bibliography* (1956), Williams expresses the belief that *Timon* was set by Folio compositors "from a fair transcript made by the same scribe who prepared the manuscript from which the folio text of *Coriolanus* was set."[24]

A variation of Williams' theory is presented by H. J. Oliver, who, in the new Arden *Timon* (1959), suggests that part of the copy of *Timon* was Shakespeare's own foul papers, and that another part was a transcript made by Ralph Crane. The Crane transcripts—parts of Shakespeare's foul papers "too 'foul' for a compositor easily to read"—correspond roughly to portions of the play of which Shakespeare's authorship had been questioned,[25] that is, I.i.176–end; I.ii; III.ii, iii, iv and v; IV.iii, part, including 461–end; V.i–end:

> If indeed the copy was in two hands, in some such division as that very tentatively suggested above, then it may be that there is also a bibliographical explanation of the two spellings of "Ventidius" and "Apemantus": I suggest that Crane wrote "Venti(d)gius" and "Apermantus" where Shakespeare wrote "Ventid-(d)ius" and "Apemantus."[26]

In *Shakespeare Quarterly* (1961), E. A. J. Honigmann also subscribes to "the view that 'two hands' were concerned with the copy for *Timon,* originally suggested by the late Philip Williams."[27] Honigmann sees the hands as those of two compositors:

> Variations in the spelling of Apemantus are the first clue. On signatures gg2[a], gg3[a], gg3[b], the spelling "Apermantus" is found without exception, the speech prefix "Aper." accompanying it; on signatures gg1[b], gg2[b], sandwiched with the others, the exclusive form is "Apemantus", with the speech prefix "Ape." On gg4[a] the "Apermantus" form continues from gg3[b] in Column A, but "Apemantus" takes over in Column B, and goes on on gg4[b] with the exception of one isolated occurrence of "Apermantus" at II.ii.78. Thereafter "Apermantus" remains unchallenged. . . .
> We now come to a further variation: this same man set up "Ventidius" (gg2[a]) while the "Apemantus" compositor chose "Ventigius" (three times on gg2[b]).[28]

Variant name spellings, then, have been used to confirm each of the three major theories about the structure of the play. To Fleay, the inconsistencies confirm

instances of incoherence caused by the imperfect join-
ing of scenes written by different authors. To Greg and
Oliver, the changes in spelling are further evidence of
"loose ends" in a play which is structurally unfinished.
To Honigmann, the attribution of the responsibility
for the spellings to the printers leaves the play intact
as an atypical production of Shakespeare's. He reasons
that the inconsistent spellings do not prove "two hands"
in the writing of the play or that Shakespeare did not
carry out his artistic intention. Textual difficulties may
be "post-Shakespearian in origin":

> Even if the copy was more illegible than was cus-
> tomary, the state of the Folio text should not bias our
> attitude to the play as a whole,—it would be a great
> mistake to suppose that it proves Shakespeare's dis-
> satisfaction with his achievement.[29]

That is, Shakespeare may have intended the structure
to be very much as it is—taking into account the irregularities created by the agents of transmission. *Timon*
"may have been meant as something other than the
regular tragedy." Honigmann argues that a great dramatist would hardly bring a play to near completion "and
then wonder that it was not what he meant it to be."
An Inn-of-Court audience "would resolve many of its
difficulties, both of value and technique."[30]

If the structure is experimental, its very uniqueness
forces an emphasis on the material which demands this
special treatment. Thus Honigmann believes that the
partly episodic form of the play may be determined by
the episodic nature of the sources in Plutarch and Lucian from which Shakespeare drew his material;[31] and
Oliver, who regards *Timon* as "a most interesting experiment in dramatic technique" (though unfinished)
is interested in how, "with an absolute minimum of

chronological narrative," Shakespeare sets off against each other "the reactions of one man to different situations, and the reactions of different men to the same situation."[32] Oliver finds this technique "far in advance of its own day and very like that of certain modern novels, those of which Aldous Huxley's *Point Counter Point* is the prototype."[33] The structure, to the proponents of the experimental theory about *Timon*, is merely an extension of the meaning, into which discussions of *Timon* as an experimental form inevitably lead.

FOOTNOTES

1. Charles Gildon, "Remarks on the Plays of Shakespear," in *The Works of William Shakespear,* ed. Nicholas Rowe (London, 1710), p. 374.
2. See Chapters II, III, and IV.
3. See Chapter I.
4. *The Plays and Poems of William Shakespeare,* ed. Edmond Malone (London, 1790), VIII, 119.
5. Joseph Ritson, *Remarks Critical and Illustrative, on the Text and Notes of the Last Edition of Shakespeare* (London, 1783), pp. 153–154.
6. John Monck Mason, *Comments on the Last Edition of Shakespeare's Plays* (Dublin, 1785), p. 303.
7. A. W. Schlegel, *Lectures on Dramatic Art and Literature,* trans. John Black (London, 1846), pp. 417–418.
8. *The Complete Works of William Hazlitt,* ed. P. P. Howe (London, 1930), IV, 210.
9. Una Ellis-Fermor, *The Jacobean Drama: An Interpretation* (London, 1936), pp. 33–34.
10. *Ibid.,* p. 34.
11. A. S. Collins, *"Timon of Athens:* A Reconsideration," *RES* (April, 1946), XXII, 97.
12. *Ibid.*
13. *Ibid.,* p. 98.
14. *Ibid.,* p. 105.
15. *Ibid.,* p. 107.
16. *William Shakespeare: The Complete Works,* ed. Charles Jasper Sisson (London, 1954), p. 910.
17. *Ibid.,* p. xv.

18. Harold S. Wilson, *On the Design of Shakespearian Tragedy* (Toronto, 1957), p. 154; Peter Alexander, "*Troilus and Cressida*, 1609," *Library* (1928), IX, 267–286; E. A. J. Honigmann, "*Timon of Athens,*" *SQ* (1961), XII, 14–18.

19. Honigmann, *op. cit.*, p. 17.

20. *Ibid.*

21. *Ibid.*, p. 18.

22. Frederick Gard Fleay, *Shakespeare Manual* (London, 1878), pp. 200, 203, 204.

23. W. W. Greg, *The Editorial Problem in Shakespeare* (Oxford, 1942), p. 149.

24. Philip Williams, Jr., "New Approaches to Textual Problems in Shakespeare," *Studies in Bibliography* (1956), VIII, 6.

25. *Timon of Athens*, Arden edition, ed. H. J. Oliver (London, 1959), p. xix.

26. *Ibid.*, p. xx

27. Honigmann, *op. cit.*, p. 18.

28. *Ibid.*, pp. 18–19.

29. *Ibid.*, pp. 19–20.

30. *Ibid.*, p. 15.

31. *Ibid.*, pp. 3–13.

32. Oliver, *op. cit.*, pp. xlviii–xlix.

33. *Ibid.*, p. xlviii. Previously, Harold Wilson had seen resemblances in theme between *Timon* and Huxley's *Brave New World*. (Harold S. Wilson, *On the Design of Shakespearian Tragedy* [Toronto, 1958]), p. 146.

Part Two
MEANING

VI

NOBLE TIMON: *Classical and Romantic Studies*

I have, in this rough work, shaped out a man. (I.i)

Most of the critics of *Timon of Athens* have been interested primarily in the structure of the play. Assuming that *Timon* should have a plot consisting of an ordered interconnection of events, most critics have decided that this causal interrelation does not exist and that therefore, the structure of the play is incoherent. Since the structure conveys the meaning, it is almost inevitable that critics who find the structure incoherent will find the meaning inconsistent. For a play regarded as structurally incoherent and meaningless, few critics have a kind word, or many words of any kind.

Some critics, however, have been interested in the meaning of the play. Their interest has been either in partial or total meanings. By "partial" meaning, I have in mind the "beauties" or moral aphorisms, or the special studies, generally not limited to *Timon* alone, designed to add to the background knowledge of the

Jacobean world. The appreciators of "beauties" in
Timon include John Cotgrave,[1] James Drake,[2] Charles
Gildon,[3] Alexander Pope,[4] and William Dodd.[5] The
investigators of special themes include Paul A. Jorgensen (militarism),[6] Lawrence Babb (melancholy),[7] Madeleine Doran and W. E. Merchant (aesthetics),[8] and Middleton Murry (biography).[9] The "total" meaning of
the play has been considered either in terms of (1) its
moral instruction (2) its study of idealism, or (3) its
thematic study of men who are "lords and owners of
their faces" and who recognize the nothingness of
earthly values. Attention here will be directed primarily to the critics of the total meaning of the play.

Because the moral instruction is given in lines
spoken by characters, critics interested in the moral instruction in *Timon* naturally think of it in terms of
the characters in the play. Of Timon's reception of
Alcibiades in the woods (IV.iii.50–117), Charles Gildon
writes that "The Scene betwixt him, *Alcibiades,* and
Timandra, &c. is full of wholesome Satire against Whor-
ing &c." And again, "The Play is full of Moral Reflections and Useful Satire. The Characters are well
mark'd and observ'd."[10] These "Moral and Instructive"
traits are, according to James Drake, "generally known
and approved" by everyone.[11] Nicholas Rowe finds
Apemantus an imitation of what a man should not be:
an example of "ill Nature and satyrical Snarling."[12]

Eighteenth- and early nineteenth-century critics
who commented on the moral instruction afforded by
Timon generally felt that it lay in the warning given by
the "ostentatious liberality" of the protagonist. These
critics include Alexander Pope, Samuel Johnson,
George Steevens, Edmond Malone, Nathan Drake, and
Henry Hallam. Much later, another critic, Elmer Stoll,
saw Timon as ostentatiously liberal, but was without

interest in the moral lesson the character might afford. Stoll's criticism was essentially objective and neoclassical. A more detailed examination of this criticism follows.

First, Alexander Pope presumably saw the meaning of the play as centering in the ostentatious liberality of the principal character. Pope's view can only be ascertained indirectly, because in his edition of Shakespeare's *Works* (1723), Pope does not consider the meaning of *Timon* beyond marking scattered instances of "beauties." However, in his poem addressed to the Earl of Burlington (1731), Pope uses the characteristics of Timon to satirize ostentatious liberality:

> At Timon's villa let us pass a day
> Where all cry out, "What sums are thrown away!"[13]

Instead of banquets held in "a Genial room," Timon's take place in "a Temple, a Hecatomb," where "What his hard heart denies/His charitable Vanity supplies."[14]

In praising the play as an instrument for the moral improvement of society, Samuel Johnson damns the "ostentatious liberality" of the principal character:

> The incidents are natural, and the characters various and exact. The catastrophe affords a very powerful warning against the ostentatious liberality, which scatters bounty, but confers no benefits, and buys flattery, but not friendship.[15]

Johnson indicates that whereas the moral lesson to be derived from the play is "powerful," the character of Timon himself is weak. For instance, to Timon's lines (I.ii.18–19), "If our betters play at that game, we must not dare/To imitate them:/Faults that are rich are fair," Johnson comments, "The whole is a trite and ob-

vious thought, uttered by Timon with a kind of affected modesty."[16] To Timon's lines (I.i.107–108),
" 'Tis not enough to help the feeble up,/But to support
him after. Fare you well," Johnson observes, "This
thought is better expressed by Dr. *Madden* in his elegy
on Archbishop *Boulter.*"[17]—to which observation,
Steevens retorted: "It has been said that Dr. Johnson
was paid ten guineas by Dr. Madden for correcting this
poem."[18]

Taking a somewhat more tolerant view of the character of Timon than did Johnson, George Steevens sees
Timon as someone who, "although beggar'd through
want of prudence, consoles himself with the reflection
that his ruin was not brought on by the pursuit of
guilty pleasures."[19] Still, characteristic of neoclassical
criticism of the play, Steevens' only comment on meaning has to do with a flaw in Timon's character.

To Malone, also, the meaning of the play lay in the
moral instruction furnished by flaws in Timon's character. In Malone's opinion, these flaws are:

> 1. That boundless prodigality which his Steward so
> forcibly describes and laments; and 2. his becoming
> a *Misanthrope,* and abjuring the society of all men
> for the crimes of a few.[20]

Not only is "boundless liberality" the major flaw to
Malone, but also to Nathan Drake and to Henry Hallam. In *Shakspeare and His Times* (1817), Drake quotes
Johnson's opinion of the "powerful lesson" afforded by
this flaw and adds, "Timon prefers the applause of the
world to the silent approval of his own conscience."[21]
Similarly, Henry Hallam (1837) writes of Timon's generosity "more from wanton ostentation than love of
others."[22]

By Hallam's time, the concept of moral instruction

as an important criterion for judging the meaning and merit of a play had been discarded. Those who still studied the characterization objectively as an imitation of life saw only Timon's weaknesses, but these weaknesses no longer conveyed any meaning except that the play had an ineffectual protagonist and consequently, not much meaning at all. For instance, H. A. Evans, editor of the *Henry Irving Shakespeare* (1890), saw Timon as someone who drew a false deduction about humanity from an unscientific sampling. Since Timon's experience had a particular rather than a general application, Shakespeare had failed to achieve universality in the play.[23] Elmer Stoll (1940) writes that Timon's emotions "are in excess of the occasion" and that Timon is the cause of his own undoing.[24]

Editors who have used the Romantic critical approach to *Timon* have generally studied the protagonist to decide whether Shakespeare's mind was functioning effectively or ineffectively when he created the character of Timon. Such editors or critics have tended to look on Timon as an ideal projection of Shakespeare himself confronting the real world. To these critics, the play is meaningful as a case history of the struggle of the soul of Everyman to reconcile object and value. Some Romantic critics, however, have seen Timon as an extension of Shakespeare's mind at a time when Shakespeare's attitude toward life was distorted for unknown reasons. Critics with this view are inclined to think that *Timon* is an unfortunate addition to the Shakespeare canon.

Editors who have shared the Romantic admiration for Timon as an idealist include Charles Knight, Samuel Singer, Henry Hudson, and Grant White. With the exception of Singer, these editors have believed that *Timon* was written by two or more authors, but that Shakespeare wrote all or most of the lines of the pro-

tagonist. Critics who have admired Timon as Shakespeare's creation of an ideal character are Hazlitt,
Lamb, Ulrici, Swinburne, presumably Tennyson, and
much more recently, G. Wilson Knight. (Schiller's
Southey's, and Leigh Hunt's admiration for Timon will
be referred to in Chapter VIII on the staging of the
play.)

In his edition of *Timon* in *The Pictorial Shakspere*
(1839), Charles Knight observes that Shakespeare completely remodeled the character of Timon from the
"beastly" Timon of tradition,[25] an observation confirmed more than one hundred years later in the detailed research of the Timon tradition by Willard
Farnham.[26] Knight also anticipates by more than a
century the critical interest, re-initiated by Una Ellis-
Fermor, in Timon as a character in isolation.[27] Knight
states that having created the character of Timon,
Shakespeare "left it standing apart in its naked power
and majesty without much regard to what surrounded
it."[28] To Knight, Timon is an ideal figure "without
any special affections," and since Timon is an ideal,
"his philanthropy passes without any violence into the
extreme of universal hatred to mankind."[29]

Samuel Singer opposes Johnson's dictum that
Timon is "a powerful lesson against ostentatious liberality." Timon is an ideal figure who thinks more of
the pleasure of his guests than of his own pleasure;
who is principally interested in kind and good actions;
who is neither dissolute nor intemperate; who has performed "great deeds" for the Athenians, for which they
are ungrateful. Seeing the ingratitude towards Timon
from Shakespeare's point of view, Singer writes:

> Shakspere seems to have entered entirely into the
> feelings of bitterness which such conduct was likely

to awaken in a good and susceptible nature, and has expressed it with vehemence and force.[30]

Henry Norman Hudson also regards Timon as a representation of ideal character confronting the world of reality. Timon's liberality "proceeds from an ideal and perhaps somewhat self-willed view of man-kind. . . . And because his love thus proceeds upon ideal grounds, therefore, when the revulsion comes, he is equally undiscriminating and self-willed in his hate."[31] Hudson sees *Timon* as an expression of Shake-speare's own feelings, "when, for some unknown cause, the Poet's mind seems to have dwelt, with a sort of melancholy, self-brooding earnestness, among the darker issues of human life and passion, as if his spirit were haunted and oppressed by the mystery of evil as resid-ing in the heart of man."[32] Because the drama is an expression of Shakespeare's melancholy state of mind, Hudson defines it as "Gothic or Romantic."[33]

Like Knight, Singer, and Hudson, Richard Grant White describes *Timon* as Shakespeare's personal search into the uneasy relationship between a man's ideals and the real world: "Difficult as it is to trace Shakespeare himself in his plays, we can hardly err in concluding that there must have been in his experience of life and in the condition of his mind some reason for his pro-duction within three years and with no intermediate relief, of three such plays as those in question."[34] (The plays were *Measure for Measure, King Lear,* and *Timon.*) The character of Timon has meaning because "Few thinking men have reached the age of thirty-five with the germs of a Timonic misanthropy undeveloped in their souls."[35]

The first English critic of the Romantic period to take a decidedly favorable view of Timon as an ideal

character was William Hazlitt.[36] The "pure soul" of
Timon, suffering from the harsh materialism of the
real world is a strikingly different figure from Johnson's
"ostentatious" prodigal, receiving his just punishment
from the world. But Hazlitt is not looking at the character objectively for evidence of verisimilitude but subjectively and sympathetically for evidence of the touch
of Shakespeare's pen. Hazlitt finds that Timon "neither
loves to abhor himself nor others":

> All his vehement misanthropy is forced, up-hill
> work. From the slippery turns of fortune, from the
> turmoils of passion and adversity, he wishes to sink
> into the quiet of the grave.[37]

To Hazlitt, as to many Romantic critics, Timon is not
a case history of a man in whom concupiscible and
irascible passions, in turn, predominate, but a history
of an ideal character who "does not utter an impreca-
tion without betraying the extravagant workings of disappointment, of love altered to hate."[38]

Charles Lamb's high regard for *Timon* is shown
by his selection of the play as one of six which he chose
to condense and simplify for the *Tales* (1817) written
with Mary.[39] Like Hazlitt, Lamb sees Timon as an
ideal being, created by Shakespeare. Timon has "a free
and prodigal nature," and is one who weighs "his
friends' affection with his own." Timon is "credulous"—
not in the derogatory sense—but "trusting."

Even after the loss of his fortune, Timon's faith in
his friends continues, when, "with a cheerful look, as if
confident of trial," he dispatches messengers to those
whom he has enriched by his prodigality. But "the
same tongues which had been loudest in his praises were
not ashamed to censure that very bounty as folly."
Timon, the idealist, quickly becomes "sick of this false
world." Although he finally admits that the world con-

tains "one honest man" (his Steward), still, "being in the shape and form of a man he could not look upon his man's face without abhorrence."[40] Lamb does not rule out the possibility that Timon committed suicide—"finished his life by violence"—but, typical of the Romantic lovers of Timon, he sees Timon's self-destructive urge as occasioned by Timon's inability to bear his humanity mirrored in the faults of others rather than as a recognition of his own flaws.[41]

Rather than a classical "imitation" of a man with the flaw of prodigality, designed to "instruct," Timon is to Lamb a projection of his creator's sad recognition that in this world idealism is self-destructive.

Ulrici tries to explain this self-destructive nature of Timon's idealism:

> But as this ideal love of man was alone the element of his life, a no less ideal misanthropy was an atmosphere of poison to him; and he was therefore of necessity the victim of his annihilating rage against himself and all mankind.[42]

To Ulrici, Timon is a study of what man *"ought* to be." An understanding of Timon's character is essential "to obtain an insight into the profound meaning of this wonderful drama":

> That common sense which laughs in pity at such idealists, is in truth the poorest and most prosaic worldly wisdom, whose treasure of experience, on which it prides itself, makes its possessor the poorer and more needy by every increase.[43]

The "meaning" of the drama appears to be that he who loses his life shall find it. Timon, who loses his life, is characterized as follows:

> To idealize is the vital principle of his mental activity. Thus has he idealized himself first of all,

> not subjectively only, but likewise objectively; his
> *acts* are in perfect conformity with his thoughts. . . .
> This idealizing humour, this exuberance of fancy and
> feeling, bring him eventually to a complete knowl-
> edge *of himself*.[44]

In sum:

> *Timon of Athens* forms the beautiful close of
> Shakespeare's poetical career. It reflects more clearly
> than any other piece, the poet's consciousness of the
> nothingness of human life and nature in themselves,
> and a Christian reliance on God, as the source of all
> that is abiding and permanent.[45]

In the above quotations, Ulrici clearly reveals his
belief in absolute values, and characteristic of Romantic
critics, he searches for these objective and absolute
values in Timon himself, a search differing from the
neoclassical study of the character of Timon only in
being broader in scope.

Like Ulrici, Swinburne, in his search for absolute
values in the play, sees Timon as a sacrificial victim, a
pre-Christ figure, a man who refuses to take into account the limitations of matter in the laws of nature.
His death is "the martyrdom of an atheistic Stylites":

> Timon is doubtless a man of far nobler type than
> any monomaniac of the tribe of Macarius, but his
> immeasurable superiority in spiritual rank to the her-
> mit fathers of the desert serves merely to make him
> a thought madder and a grain more miserable than
> the whole thebaid of Christomaniacs rolled into one.[46]

We know indirectly that Tennyson shared the Romantic regard for the protagonist of the play. Signing
himself "Timon," Bulwer-Lytton had criticized Tennyson for appearing on Peel's pension list. In reply,

Tennyson wrote "Timon," an eleven-stanza poem which appeared in *Punch,* February 28, 1846. Two stanzas from Tennyson follow:

> We know him, out of Shakespeare's art,
>   And those fine curses which he spoke;
> The old Timon, with his noble heart,
>   That, strongly loathing, greatly broke.
>
> A TIMON you! Nay, nay, for shame:
>   It looks too arrogant a jest—
> The fierce old man—to take his name,
>   You bandbox. Off, and let him rest![47]

A modern counterpart of the Romantic admiration for Timon as an ideal figure is found in the criticism of G. Wilson Knight.[48] Knight says much the same things about Timon which Ulrici said, but Knight says them in a more rhetorical way. Just as Ulrici saw Timon's acts as "in perfect conformity with his thoughts," so Knight sees Timon as someone who "will tolerate no disorder within and without his mind."[49] But Knight's description of Timon as an ideal of love and hate is far more ecstatic than Ulrici's:

> There is no tragic movement so swift, so clean-cut, so daring and so terrible in all Shakespeare as this Timon. We pity Lear, we dread for Macbeth: but the awfulness of Timon, dwarfing pity and out-topping sympathy, is as the grandeur and menace of the naked rock of a sky-lifted mountain, whither we look and tremble. Deserting Athens, he steps from time into eternity. The world of humanity tilts over, and is reversed. We see now, not with the aspiring Spirit of Love that has scorned mankind forever. . . . Thus Timon preserves the grander harmony of loneliness and universal loathing, and fronts his destiny, emperor still in mind and soul, wearing the imperial

> nakedness of Hate. This unswerving majesty is a
> grander thing than the barbaric fury of Othello, or
> the faltering ire of Lear. The heart's gold in Timon
> has seen the ungrateful and miserly greed that would
> coin for use the infinite of a great soul's love.[50]

This "miserly greed that would coin for use the
infinite of a great soul's love," resembles the greedy
worldly wisdom, observed by Ulrici, who wrote of it
that it "makes its possessor the poorer and more needy
by every increase."[51] In comparing the criticism of
Ulrici, who epitomized Romantic criticism of Timon,
with the criticism of Knight, we see no difference except in amplification. In his criticism of Timon, Knight
is a rhetorical Romantic.

Most of the critics who looked on the character of
Timon as a reflection of Shakespeare's creative genius
saw Timon as a successful study of idealism. But two
"Romantic" critics, Thomas Campbell and A. W.
Schlegel, were unhappy with Timon as a principal
character. They felt that Shakespeare had somehow
failed to help the playgoer, through Timon, to arrive
at an understanding of idealism through experience.
The Romantic ideal, in Robert Langbaum's definition,
must perceive "not only that the world is alive but that
the spirit pervading it is good."[52] Timon is not an ideal
because in undergoing the extremes of human experience, he fails to reconcile object and value—or so Campbell and Schlegel reason. Campbell refers to Timon
not as an ideal but as someone who has, by hate so extreme that it forces him to reject the society of man,
actually lowered himself on the chain of being. He is
"a human mad-dog."[53] Campbell's impression is that
the deficiency in characterization grows out of a deficiency in Shakespeare's own understanding, that it is
"far from displaying Shakespeare improved either in
his philosophy or his philanthropy."[54]

Schlegel goes into more precise detail on Timon's failure to reconcile object and value:

> Timon was a fool in his generosity; in his discontent he is a madman; he is everywhere wanting in the wisdom which enables a man in all things to observe the due measure. Although the truth of his extravagant feelings is proved by his death, and though when he digs up a treasure he spurns the wealth which seems to tempt him, we yet see distinctly enough that the vanity of wishing to be singular, in both the parts that he plays, had some share in his liberal self-forgetfulness, as well as in his anchoritical seclusion.[55]

Timon never arrives at an understanding of idealism through experience: he "frets himself to death."

Coleridge believed that intellect, not emotion, stimulated Shakespeare's creative imagination while composing *Timon*.[56] But the perfect fusion of object and value takes place through the emotions, not the intellect. Therefore, Coleridge relegated *Timon* to a secondary position—"a Lear of domestic or ordinary life":

> ——a local eddy of passion on the high road of society, while all around is the week-day goings on of wind and weather; a Lear, therefore, without its soul-searching flashes, its ear-cleaving thunderclaps, its meteoric splendors—without the contagion and the fearful sympathies of nature, the fates, the furies, the frenzied elements, dancing in and out, now breaking through, and scattering—now hand in hand with—the fierce or fantastic group of human passions, crimes, and anguishes, reeling on the unsteady ground, in a wild harmony to the shock and swell of an earthquake.[57]

Interestingly, Coleridge, using a Romantic subjective measure for judging the play, comes almost to the same conclusion about it as have critics who have used a classical objective measure. Coleridge's decision that the

play is "a local eddy" is close to the decision of some
neoclassicists that Timon's is a special case and that
the play fails to achieve universality.[58]

A complex mixture of Romantic and neoclassical
criticism characterizes some of the critical comment
about *Timon,* for instance, that of D. A. Traversi, Louis
Cazamian, Mark Van Doren, and Hardin Craig.
Traversi finds that whereas Lear's suffering is "a con-
centration of that of man in general," Timon is "too
isolated in his suffering."[59] The characterization of Lear
has more universal meaning. Traversi looks at characterization objectively but at plot subjectively as "an
extension of the poetry," or "an expanded image of an
experience which the poet, following the promptings of
his creative impulse, is concerned to mould into artistic form."[60]

The unreality of the characters is stressed in the
criticism of Cazamian, Van Doren, and Craig. To Louis
Cazamian, Timon is a character in a Jonsonian comedy
of humors. Timon's "humour"—that because of his
generosity his friends will come to his assistance—is not
noble, but "risible."[61] At the same time, the play "ap-
partient probablement aux confessions déguisées par
lesquelles le Shakespeare inconnu s'est ouvert un
chemin vers la sérénité."[62]

Mark Van Doren finds that "Timon is not so much
a man as a figure. . . . Our fears for him are not real.
Neither is our pity for him real."[63] The "intrinsic interest" in the play lies in "the limit of pessimism it
reaches." Having complained of the failure of the play
to produce Aristotelian *catharsis,* Van Doren adds a
more subjective criticism: "One is free to conjecture
that in Timon's tomb Shakespeare buried his own bit-
terness."[64]

Hardin Craig complains that Timon is less than

human. "Timon belongs, according to species, to a third class. He does not know about the race, mistakes a part for the whole, wakes up too late, and gets out of bed on the wrong side."[65] The meaning of Timon's experience appears to be that "Hospitality and liberality are golden virtues, men are too base to appreciate them, shame on them!" Obviously, Craig is looking for an absolute value in the play. It is this search which distinguishes him from some other critics whose opinions of Timon will be considered in the next chapter.

With Craig's objective criticism of the play's failure to please and to instruct, and of the characters' verisimilitude—there is a "mechanical quality" about the minor characters—Craig combines a subjective criticism of the play as a creation of Shakespeare. How did Shakespeare come to write this "sort of orphan not fitting in with any groupings of plays?" The answer lies in Shakespeare's state of mind. "There was disillusionment in the mind of Shakespeare when he wrote *King Lear*. It is just possible that it carried over into *Timon of Athens*."[66] This view is seconded by David Cook.[67]

To summarize, up to this point, the meaning of the play, the classicists generally saw it as being a warning against ostentatious liberality; the Romanticists saw it as projecting an ideal figure—to be emulated (Ulrici *et al.*) or shunned (Schlegel *et al.*). Critics who made a combined classical-Romantic judgment found the play dissatisfying (Cazamian *et al.*), the reason being that these critics first judged the play negatively from the classical point of view as lacking universality, verisimilitude, or proper moral instruction, and then attempted to attribute these weaknesses to the unfortunate state of Shakespeare's mind. Both classical and Romantic critics were making an objective search for some absolute value in *Timon*. The idea that such value it-self might not exist and that the very unreality of the play might be a virtue would appear only after critics had begun to apply the concept of relativity to litera-ture. Partly influenced by the image studies, a new ap-proach to the criticism of Shakespeare's plays, notably the criticism of *Coriolanus*, *Measure for Measure*, *Troilus and Cressida*, and *Timon*, became evident in the 1930's. This approach, which I shall call the "the-matic" approach, because the criticism is concerned with themes rather than with truths, will be discussed in the next chapter.

FOOTNOTES

1. John Cotgrave, *The English Treasury of Wit and Lan-guage* (London, 1655). *Timon* is second only to *Hamlet* as a source for the "beauties" which Cotgrave discovers and lists under the headings, "Of Ceremony, Complement" (p. 39), "Of Compassion" (p. 49), "Of Delay, Deliberation" (p. 75), "Of Duells" (p. 87), "Of Friendship" (p. 113), "Of Ingratitude" (p. 148), "Of Old Age" (p. 205), "Of Ranting &c." (p. 210), "Of Prodigality" (p. 237), and "Of Theft &c." (p. 234). But as Ger-ald Eades Bentley has shown in "John Cotgrave's *English Trea-sury of Wit and Language* and the Elizabethan Drama," *SP* (April, 1943), XL, 198, this large percentage of quotations from *Timon* is no indication of the play's popularity.
2. James Drake, *The Antient and Modern Stages survey'd* (London, 1699), p. 206.
3. Charles Gildon, "Remarks on the Plays of Shakespear," in *The Works of Mr. William Shakespear*, ed. Nicholas Rowe (London, 1710), VII, 374–375.
4. *The Works of Shakespear*, ed. Alexander Pope (1725), V. Pope uses commas to denote "the most shining passages," as II.ii.213–222 (p. 33), VI.i.1–33 (p. 54), IV.ii. 10–17 (p. 56), IV.iii.31–45 (p. 58), IV.iii.108–114 (p. 61), IV.iii.178–196 (pp. 63–64), IV.iii.222–232 (p. 65), IV.iii.250–274 (p. 66), and IV.iii.330–348 (p. 68).
5. William Dodd, *The Beauties of Shakspeare* (London, 1825), pp. 322–334.

6. Paul A. Jorgensen, *Shakespeare's Military World* (Berkeley and Los Angeles, 1956), pp. 21, 23, 29, 191–196, 203, 208, 266–267, 279–292.

7. Lawrence Babb, *The Elizabethan Malady: A Study of Melancholia in English Literature From 1580 to 1642* (East Lansing, 1951), pp. 91–96.

8. Madeleine Doran, *Endeavors of Art: A Study of Form in Elizabethan Drama* (Madison, 1954), pp. 72–74; W. M. Merchant, "*Timon* and the Conceit of Art," *SQ* (1953), VI, 249–257.

9. John Middleton Murry, *Shakespeare* (London, 1936), pp. 93–94, 113, 342.

10. Gildon, *op. cit.*, p. 375.

11. James Drake, *The Antient and Modern Stages survey'd, or Mr. Collier's View of the Immorality and Profaness of the English Stage Set in a True Light* (London, 1699), p. 206.

12. *The Works of Mr. William Shakespear*, ed. Nicholas Rowe (London, 1709), I, xix.

13. *The Works of Alexander Pope*, eds. Whitewell Elwin and William J. Courthope (London, 1871), III, 179.

14. *Ibid.*, p. 183.

15. *The Plays of William Shakespeare*, ed. Samuel Johnson (London, 1765), VI, 276.

16. *Ibid.*, pp. 181–182.

17. *Ibid.*, p. 173.

18. *The Plays and Poems of William Shakespeare*, eds. James Boswell and Edmond Malone (London, 1821), XIII, 260.

19. *The Plays of Shakespeare*, eds. Samuel Johnson, George Steevens, and Isaac Reed (London, 1793), XI, 525.

20. *The Plays and Poems of William Shakespeare*, ed. Edmond Malone (London, 1790), VIII, 136.

21. Nathan Drake, *Shakspeare and His Times* (London, 1817), II, 447.

22. Henry Hallam, *Introduction to the Literature of Europe* (London, 1837), II, 567–568.

23. *The Henry Irving Shakespeare. Timon of Athens*, ed. H. A. Evans (New York, 1890), VII, 3–13.

24. Elmer Edgar Stoll, *Shakespeare and Other Masters* (Cambridge, Mass., 1940), pp. 20, 275.

25. *The Pictorial Edition of the Works of Shakspere*, ed. Charles Knight (London, 1839), V, 338.

26. Willard Farnham, *Shakespeare's Tragic Frontier: The World of His Final Tragedies* (Berkeley and Los Angeles, 1950), pp. 39–77.

27. Una Ellis-Fermor, "*Timon of Athens*: An Unfinished Play," *RES* (July, 1942), XVIII, 282.

28. Knight, *op. cit.*, p. 337.
29. *Ibid.*, p. 341.
30. *The Dramatic Works of William Shakespeare*, ed. Samuel Weller Singer (Cheswick, 1826), VIII, 2.
31. *The Works of Shakespeare*, ed. H. N. Hudson (Boston, 1872), VIII, 18–19.
32. *Ibid.*, p. 6.
33. H. N. Hudson, *Lectures of Shakspeare* (New York, 1848), I, 147.
34. Richard Grant White, *Studies in Shakespeare* (Boston, 1899), p. 211.
35. *The Works of William Shakespeare*, ed. Richard Grant White (Boston, 1875), X, 197.
36. *The Complete Works of William Hazlitt*, ed. P. P. Howe (London, 1930), IV, 210–213.
37. *Ibid.*, p. 213.
38. *Ibid.*, p. 212.
39. *The Works of Charles and Mary Lamb*, ed. Thomas Hutchinson (Oxford, 1924), II, 183–195.
40. *Ibid.*, p. 191.
41. *Ibid.*, p. 185. For the latter view, that if Timon commits suicide as expiation, he achieves tragic stature, see Bernard Paulin, *Études Anglaises* (1964) XVII, No. 1, 8.
42. Hermann Ulrici, *Shakspeare's Dramatic Art*, trans. Alexander J. W. Morrison (London, 1846), p. 241.
43. *Ibid.*, p. 240.
44. *Ibid.*
45. *Ibid.*, p. 244.
46. Algernon Charles Swinburne, *A Study of Shakespeare* (New York, 1880), p. 213.
47. Alfred Tennyson, *Poetic and Dramatic Works* (Cambridge, Mass., 1898), p. 791. Professor Arthur Kyle Davis called this reference of *Timon* to my attention.
48. G. Wilson Knight, *The Wheel of Fire* (London, 1930), pp. 232–260.
49. *Ibid.*, p. 242.
50. *Ibid.*
51. Ulrici, *op. cit.*, p. 240.
52. Robert Langbaum, *The Poetry of Experience* (London, 1957), p. 17.
53. Thomas Campbell, "Remarks on the Life and Writings of William Shakespeare," *Lives of British Dramatists,* eds. Thomas Campbell, *et al.* (Philadelphia, 1846), p. 87.
54. *Ibid.*
55. A. W. Schlegel, *Lectures on Dramatic Art and Literature,* trans. John Black (London, 1846), p. 418. Similar criticism of

Timon's "inordinate love of distinction" had been expressed in the eighteenth century by William Richardson in his *Essays on Shakespeare's Dramatic Character* (London, 1785).

56. Samuel Taylor Coleridge, *Lectures and Notes on Shakespeare and Other Dramatists* (Oxford, 1931), p. 75.

57. *Ibid.*, pp. 134–135.

58. Evans (New York, 1890) *op. cit.*

59. D. A. Traversi, *An Approach to Shakespeare* (New York, 1956), p. 192.

60. *Ibid.*, p. 181.

61. Louis Cazamian, *L'Humour de Shakespeare* (Paris, 1945), p. 173.

62. *Ibid.*, p. 172.

63. Mark Van Doren, *Shakespeare* (New York, 1939), p. 250.

64. *Ibid.*, p. 253.

65. Hardin Craig, *An Interpretation of Shakespeare* (New York, 1948), pp. 247–248.

66. *Ibid.*, p. 248.

67. David Cook, "Timon of Athens," *Shakespeare Survey* 16 (1963), 94.

VII

LIVELIER THAN LIFE: *Imagery and "Thematic" Studies*

*Our poesy is as a gum, which oozes/
From whence 'tis nourisht.* (I.i)

A T the time that studies of imagery began to receive marked critical attention—in the 1930's—*Timon of Athens* had lost what little literary reputation it had gained during the Romantic period. The theorists who were convinced of the divided authorship of the play had gone over it so thoroughly looking for inconsistencies in the plot, bad poetry, and trite thought that, among them, virtually none of the play was attributed to Shakespeare. Often, the play was not alluded to in works of Shakespeare criticism, or at most, was given passing and derogatory mention in connection with another play. In 1917, J. M. Robertson had announced that he was able to "clinch the hypothesis" that Chapman "had a main hand in the play."[1] In 1924, H. Dugdale Sykes had decided that *Timon* was "a hasty and perfunctory revision" by Shakespeare of a play by Day and Middleton.[2]

Soon after these theorists of divided authorship had

torn the play apart, the students of imagery began the search for image clusters and key metaphors running through the play. Since these image patterns occurred in the "non-Shakespearean" as well as the "Shakespearean" portions of *Timon,* the image studies served to tie the play together. Although undoubtedly influenced by the critical background against which they worked—the theories that the play was only partly Shakespeare's or unfinished—the students of imagery were forced to conclude that consistent patterns indicated that more of the play was Shakespeare's and that more of it was complete than had been supposed.

To some extent, the image studies were descendants of the neoclassical studies of "flowers of rhetoric." New blood had been added to the study through the Romantic influence. That is, the image patterns were studied, not objectively, but as part of Shakespeare's plan. An ancestor of image study is recognizable in Robert Gould's *The Play-House* (1685), when Gould writes that "In *Timon, Lear, The Tempest,* we may find/Vast Images of thy unbounded mind."[3] Although Gould's images have more to do with *Timon* as a totality, they also include rhetorical effects. Warburton (1747) was interested in consistency of imagery in *Timon* and used it as a principle on which to determine some of his emendations.[4] Warburton's conception of consistent imagery extended only through a passage, however, rather than an entire play. For example, he emends "levell'd malice" (I.i.48) to "leven'd malice" on the grounds that it would render the imagery in the passage more consistent, "leven'd" being "a proper epithet for the acidity of that passion," which suits well with "infects" and "leaving no tract behind" (line 51), as, writes Warburton, "anything fermenting or corrosive does."[5]

Closely related to consistent imagery in developing

an idea was the Elizabethan play upon words, whereby
an argument advanced by a series of verbal quibbles.
F. P. Wilson pointed out that an eighteenth-century
critic, Walter Whiter, studied these progressions in a
book "which anticipates in a most interesting way much
modern work on Shakespeare's imagery."⁶ Basing his
work on Locke's doctrine of the association of ideas,
Whiter reasoned that many of the trains of associated
images were not deliberately produced by Shakespeare
but emanated from his unconscious mind. Whiter began his investigations with the following passage in
Timon:

                              What, think'st
    That the bleak air, thy boisterous chamberlain,
    Will put thy shirt on warm? Will these moist trees,
    That have outlived the eagle, page thy heels,
    And skip when thou point'st out?
                                    (IV.iii.221–225)

Hanmer emended "moist" trees to "moss'd" trees, as
have major editors since Hanmer, with the exception
of Johnson, Charles Knight, Collier in his first (1842)
edition, Munro, Oliver, and Charney. Whiter argued
that Shakespeare unconsciously associated the idea of a
chamberlain putting a "warm" or "aired" shirt on his
master with the opposite idea of "moist" or "unaired."⁷
      Whiter also pointed out the recurrent association of
candy and fawning dogs in *Timon* and other plays of
Shakespeare's, notably *Antony and Cleopatra*. But
Whiter's work received little attention. Caroline
Spurgeon rediscovered the candy-fawning dogs nexus
in *Timon* in 1935:

      What do we find is the central image, the picture
    constantly before Shakespeare's eyes in this play?

Dogs: dogs fawning and eating and lapping and
licking, with 'gluttonous maws' devouring their lord's
meat; hounds feasting on the blood of the animal
they have killed; dogs being given food denied to
men, dogs licking up remnants; dogs being stoned and
spurned and kicked; a mangy dog, a sleeping dog,
an unpeaceable dog, a beggar's dog.

 Even Timon's imprecations are coloured by this
picture, which is ever with him: 'Destruction *fang*
mankind', he cries,
 And may diseases *lick up* their false bloods!
and the thought of Flavius is likewise tinged with it.
Why, he asks the servants of his ruined lord's creditors,
did you not submit your bills,
 When your false masters eat of my lord's meat?
 Then they could smile and *fawn upon* his debts,
 And take down the interest into their *gluttonous
maws.*

* * *

 [Timon] proceeds to expound his own position in
a passionate speech. It opens with 'dog' and ends
with 'flatter'd', but had we not the key of the earlier
group of images we should scarcely realise that it also
is shot through with the picture of dogs licking sweets,
and with their mouths and tongues melting the iced
sugar on cake or sweetmeats.[8]

 Miss Spurgeon observes that the fact that these
images are "as clearly and characteristically Shakespeare's as if he had signed his name after each" helps
to establish his authorship for at least "a much larger
part of this incoherent and unsatisfactory play than has
hitherto been attributed to him."[9] In other words,
Miss Spurgeon's image studies of *Timon* directed attention to recurrent symbolic meanings in *Timon* and
helped to return more of the play to Shakespeare.

 Miss Spurgeon's study of the imagery in *Timon* was

made against a background of the work of the theorists
of divided authorship—Wright, Sykes, Parrott, and
Robertson. Wolfgang Clemen's study of the imagery
was made against a background of the work of the "unfinished" theorists, notably Una Ellis-Fermor (who in
her paper on imagery published in 1937 commended
Miss Spurgeon's and Clemen's work).[10]

Carrying the studies of Shakespeare's imagery a step
further than did Miss Spurgeon, Clemen tries to relate
the imagery to the dramatic action of each play.[11]
Clemen finds that *Timon* contains what he calls "thinking-in" images not closely related to the immediate
dramatic situation and which support the idea that the
play is not quite finished.

Clemen's thoughtful study of these images in relation to the dramatic structure of the play serves to draw
attention to the intellectual quality of *Timon*. For instance, Clemen points out that the images convey the
message that Timon himself—not merely his food—is
being eaten by false friends. He quotes, "O you gods,
what a number of men eat Timon. . . . It grieves me
to see so many dip their meat in one man's blood"
(I.ii.40–42). Or, "to drink those men/Upon whose age
we void it up again" (I.ii.143–144). Or, "I never tasted
Timon in my life" (III.ii.84), and, "Cut my heart in
sums. . . . Tell out my blood" (III.iv.93, 95).

These "thinking-in" images emphasize the "inner-
complex of representations." They are heaped up, for
example, in the first scene of Act IV, Timon's monologue outside the wall of Athens, which contains in
quick succession eighteen images and disconnected
thoughts. The wealth of imagery increases the very
moment Timon (and Lear) are thrown on their own
resources. "Their language brings inner visions to light
in the same measure as their relations to the world of

men are cut off." But whereas in *Lear* all of the reflections are closely connected with the action, in *Timon*, Clemen concludes, "there is a perceptible loosening of the firm guidance of the dramatic action."[12]

A third, less extensive study of the early 1930's of the imagery in *Timon* was that of J. W. Draper.[13] Draper's study, like the work of Miss Spurgeon and of Wolfgang Clemen, served to draw attention to the meaning of the play and to restore it to Shakespeare. Draper decided that the image patterns were Shakespeare's, and drew the conclusion that the editors of the Folio were correct in assuming that Shakespeare wrote the play.

Each critic, to paraphrase the old fable, felt a different part of the elephant and therefore, noticed new things. Whereas Miss Spurgeon noticed the sequence of images in *Timon* characteristic of other plays by Shakespeare—those of flattering friends and fawning dogs licking sweets, and Clemen noted the concept of man himself as the "meat" eaten by materialists, Draper was interested in the images of usury running through the play. He suspected that *Timon* is "a dramatic elegy on the ideals of chivalry that were succumbing in a capitalistic age."[14]

Since the parts of the play supplement each other in developing the attack on the evils of usury, Draper argues that the tests are invalid by which the play had, for more than a century, been ascribed to multiple authorship. The stylistic tests are dubious matters of taste, the inconsistencies of detail are debatable, and as for disunity of plan, this too is non-existent if the play is studied as a concerted attack on usury.

This defense of the "unity of plan" in *Timon* is indicative of the strong Romantic tinge in the studies of imagery. The theorists who had seen two or more

hands in the play were primarily interested in its structure whereas the students of imagery, like the Romantics, were primarily interested in meaning. A comment of Draper's illustrates the swing back to Ro-
manticism in the criticism of imagery:

> Although the last century of scholarship has
> doubted Shakespeare's writing of large parts of *Timon
> of Athens,* the present study leads one rather to agree
> with Hazlitt and the other earlier critics who found
> in the play a unity of design that they attributed to
> Shakespeare's hand throughout; and scholarship per-
> haps might well review its present doubts, bearing in
> mind a Jacobean Timon, a sort of liberal young Bas-
> sanio, who, without the moneyed backing of Antonio
> and Portia, experienced to his sorrow the hard eco-
> nomic facts of the Jacobean age.[15]

Besides usury, dog-candy imagery, and metaphors of
man as a sacrifice, critics were discovering several other
interrelated symbols in *Timon.* Una Ellis-Fermor
found recurrent waves of disintegration and chaos: "In
Timon's mind, the themes of disease, misgeneration,
and robbery image themselves in the elements; the
earth, the sea, and the great processes of nature."[16] One
tiny hope emerges to become stronger in the final
plays:

> The 'strong base of the world' has indeed now
> broken up, but through the rift is revealed, at depths
> almost below man's vision, a new base not dreamed
> of, where the 'perpetual sober gods' remain, untouched
> even by the 'trepidation of the spheres'. The emer-
> gence from destruction to constructive experience has
> begun again, though it may be revealed in *Timon*
> only in this one phrase.[17]

Other symbols, metaphors, or sequences of images discovered in *Timon* have been gold (R. P. Draper),[18]

dogs (Empson),[19] Timon as the sun (Holloway),[20] and beasts (Ribner[21] and Farnham).[22]

A new approach to the role of images in creating a coherent theme in *Timon* has been that of Willard Farnham, who tracks the development of the beast image in the Timon story through its earlier sources in Lucian, Plutarch, Mexia, Gruget, Boiastuau, Painter, Alday, Greene, and Barckley. Farnham's thesis is that Shakespeare enlarged on the beast imagery from his sources to such an extent that human society in *Timon* appears to have "more of beasthood than of manhood."[23]

In more detail, Farnham sees the theme as introduced in the first scene when Apemantus observes, "The strain of man's bred out/Into baboon and monkey." The theme is maintained consistently to the end of the play, when Alcibiades asks Timon in the woods to identify himself, and Timon answers, "A beast, as thou art." Throughout the play, references to human beings as beasts and to beastliness occur repeatedly. Athens is called "a forest of beasts," the soldier for whom Alcibiades pleads is said to have committed murder in "beastly fury," and the professional warfare of Alcibiades is called "beastly." The beast metaphor reaches a climax in the banquet scene in Act III, where Timon shouts to his false friends, "Uncover, dogs, and lap." Timon later denounces these friends as "affable wolves," and "meek bears." Timon goes to the woods not to live among the wolves, but to escape the wolves: "Timon will to the woods, where he shall find/Th' unkindest beast more kinder than mankind." (IV.i.35–36.) To the visiting Alcibiades, Timon says, "For thy part, I do wish thou wert a dog,/That I might love thee something."[24]

Closely related to the studies of symbolism and imagery in the play are studies which I shall call "thematic" because they have to do with the basic theme or themes. The authors of these thematic studies regard Timon as simultaneously real and ideal and the play itself as a daring and rebellious attempt on Shakespeare's part to expose publicly the private world of man in relation to men. The studies tend (1) to approach Timon through Shakespeare's mind, thus showing their kinship with Romantic studies; (2) to see Timon as a character in isolation (as did some Romantic studies);[25] (3) to consider the play experimental; and (4) to praise it for its intellectual texture as well as for any deep meaning it may convey.

Among those who have praised the intellectual-experimental theme of *Timon* have been Una Ellis-Fermor, Peter Alexander, A. S. Collins, Charles Sisson, J. C. Maxwell, H. J. Oliver, Walter Kaufmann, and E. A. J. Honigmann. Pioneering in these studies was Miss Ellis-Fermor. To her, Shakespeare intended as the theme of the play the destruction of all values and the return of chaos:

> Never did the sense of chaos, of disjunction and flying apart of the very bonds of earth, of mutiny in the spheres themselves, find as nearly apocalyptic expression as in the sequence in which *Macbeth* and *Lear* lead up to *Timon*. . . . It is the laws that integrate civilization itself, no less than those that wall in the human mind, that break apart in *Lear* and *Timon*. . . . *Timon* defines the theme that *Lear* had touched, and loses little of its magnitude in definition. . . . It is the subversion of society only that he seeks at first, but he moves step by step through the gradually unfolding experience of destruction until the boundaries of thought themselves dissolve and the mind itself, the very instrument of consciousness, is drawn out into chaos.[26]

Timon finds no foundation, but only further dissolution. "The world-order is no longer evil. There is no

longer any discernible world-order. All is resolved into
disparate, warring elements. . . . Chaos is come
again."[27]

In *Timon,* which grows out of the Jacobean "weari-
ness of spirit" at "this spectacle of universal decay and
corruption," "the unresolvable evil of the universe,"
Shakespeare has attempted an experiment: "to penetrate
and analyze something beyond expression, beyond what
can be contained in the mind of man."[28] The theme
revolves around Timon, a man stripped down to
"primeval, individual man,"[29] who has no strong rela-
tionships in the present, and shows no sign of their having moulded him in the past, who finds no foundation for security, but only further depths of dissolution,
which extend "beyond Nature's laws themselves" to
deeper reaches in which the mind itself becomes a negation, "emptied alike of properties and of cohesion."[30]

Like Una Ellis-Fermor, Peter Alexander has high
praise for the intellectual core of *Timon,* which he also
approaches from the Romantic view as an extension of
Shakespeare's mind.[31] His sympathy with Romantic
criticism of *Timon* is indicated by the favorable way in
which he presents quotations from Lamb. Like Lamb,
Alexander has great admiration for Timon himself,
whom Alexander regards as partly human, partly super-
human. Alexander warns that Apemantus' constant
criticism of Timon, accepted at face value by many
scholars, is not to be taken seriously. We must "consider the source." Apemantus is not an ordinary human being, but rather, "the world's self-love turned in-
side out."[32] The theme of the play must be interpreted
in relation to the kind of audience for which *Timon*
was probably designed. *Timon,* like *Troilus,* was con-
structed, presumably, for a sophisticated, intellectual
audience. The "intellectual appeal" of the theme lies
in the piercing of "the pretences of the world." Worldly

illusions are exposed "with an invective beyond anything in Molière's sardonic smile."[33]

The non-realistic opening of *Timon*, in which
verisimilitude is abandoned, has been noticed by various critics, especially by Miss Ellis-Fermor.[34] Using this
opening as a key to Shakespeare's purpose, A. S. Collins
examines the realistic-unrealistic nature of the entire
play.[35]

Experimental in thought and form, the play is
Shakespeare's sophisticated version of the medieval
morality play. Collins argues that there is virtually no
characterization except of Alcibiades (but his is important), and that there are no women, the Mask of Ladies
being "a mere stage property": "The characters are
subtilized Virtues and Vices, the staple of the play is
satire and argument."[36]

Reminiscent of the Romantic consideration of
Timon as an idealist is Collins' observation that Timon
is not Bounty alone, but Ideal Bounty, and as this ideal
quality may be led astray by Flattery, and may not heed
the faithful Steward, so may Timon be led astray.
Timon is isolated in a society corrupted by wealth and
selfishness. The society is false and hollow, from the
Jeweller, the flattering Lords, and the Senators to the
Old Athenian who has "bred" his daughter "at dearest
cost." Timon is not condemned for being too pure
to exist in the world. Shakespeare merely demonstrates
that his existence is not possible, or practical. Collins
acknowledges Hazlitt's priority in seeing this special
meaning of the play. In Collins' words, "Let us not see
mere stupid extravagance in Timon, but rather feel
with Yeats that 'only the wasteful virtues earn the
sun. . . .' "[37]

Collins agrees with Una Ellis-Fermor and Peter
Alexander that *Timon* was written for an academic

audience. Designed especially for such an audience, *Timon* "is such a satire upon a cold-hearted commercial community, fearfully reinforcing its security by a heartless legalism, as Mr. W. H. Auden might well have envied."[38] The great scene of the play is that of Alcibiades before the Senate (III.v). (It will be recalled that divided-authorship theorists had recommended its expurgation.) Alcibiades in this scene is Ideal Friendship, but he is also a real man. "This is the true transformation of the old morality play."[39] Finally, Collins observes of *Timon:* "This is one of the plays of Shakespeare that Francis Bacon could not have even begun to write."[40]

Similar high praise of the play as an intellectual experiment is expressed by Henri Fluchère:

> Released from the finite in evil, the Shakespearian experiment can be pursued beyond the absolute nothingness which is for Timon the sovereign good. One could not remain in this appalling emptiness after a complete repudiation of Creation and of oneself without losing one's whole sense of substantial existence. But, again, the supreme adventure had to be attempted which leads to the unimaginable so that the spirit might be renewed if life continued after the plunge into the abyss.[41]

Fluchère shares the Romantic view of Timon as a reflection of Shakespeare's mind: Timon is Shakespeare's "mouthpiece." He has, "in his immense solitude," penetrated "to the depths of despair."[42] He is a character in isolation. He knows "no personal, intimate conflict." He is "of more than human stature, and his mighty voice is like a trumpet of denunciation, sounding unbearably on the Day of Judgment."[43]

The play is unique in that "Shakespeare has gone

to the utmost limits of his tragic view of the world."
Because *Timon* is "situated outside all the psychologi-
cal crises which alone are supposed to be capable of
producing masterpieces," the play "has rarely been
given the place it deserves, among the very highest."[44]

Charles Sisson follows the procedure of Miss Ellis-
Fermor, Alexander, Collins, and Fluchère in approaching *Timon* through Shakespeare's mind, in seeing the
protagonist as a character in isolation, in finding the
play experimental, and in praising it for its theme.
First, Sisson admires the play as a creation of Shakespeare's:

> If we turn to *Timon of Athens* from Burton's
> summary of the story in *The Anatomy of Melancholy,*
> we see more clearly how it became in Shakespeare the
> vehicle for a powerful and tragic study of character,
> how he clad bare bones in flesh and blood and spirit,
> how he made Timon himself a noble, generous ideal-
> ist, whose misanthropy is one with his high minded-
> ness, who, like Hamlet, is a true prince among men.[45]

Timon is a character in isolation. As Harold Jenkins
adds in an introductory essay to Sisson's edition, Shakespeare's heroes generally progress toward some point
where all the striving and self-seeking of the world become of no account. Macbeth found that his ambition
ended by "signifying nothing." Lear became one with
the elements on the naked heath. "Nothing," says
Timon, "brings me all things," and "his spirit moves
in harmony with the everlasting forces, the waves, which
break over his tomb."[46]

According to Sisson, the play is misunderstood because it is an experimental form. It shows Shakespeare's
"new deep interest in forms of art other than the drama,
which reappears in *The Winter's Tale.*"[47] Although

Sisson regrets "the lamentable state of the text," he believes that *Timon* is "a finished play, imperfect certainly, and negligent even, upon a theme and story which did not lend itself to perfection in form, but gave scope to much splendid writing."[48] Sisson sees the play as attempting something new both artistically and also intellectually: "No play of Shakespeare requires more, and repays more, the closest attention to the precise sense of the words and thoughts."[49] The play needs this close attention because in its depiction of Timon, it is a powerful character study.

Comparable attitudes toward *Timon* to those held by Sisson, Miss Ellis-Fermor, Alexander, Collins, and Fluchère are held by Harold Wilson. Wilson also sees *Timon* as an experimental play written to stimulate an intellectual audience, a play which features a character in isolation from humanity. The play is "a great poem rather than a great play," an intimate expression of Shakespeare's creative impulse: "Shakespeare nowhere gives evidence of being unduly impressed by Aristotle's authority, and we must allow him to deviate from it for his own purposes."[50] Timon stands apart . . . "in repudiating the selfish ways of man, [he] can find peace only in death." Timon's experience is an indictment of human society, "which is exhibited, in Timon's rejection of it, as wholly corrupt." The "central dramatic conflict" is that of Timon "against the forces of moral ugliness."[51]

Wilson, and, as we shall see, Honigmann, see *Timon* and *Troilus* as experimental plays designed for an academic audience. The intellectual content is similar, a dramatization of "a state of mind":

> Each play, by reason of its unconventionality, its deliberate flouting of human complacency and self-

esteem, must have been a work to which Shakespeare
attached a special importance; else why should he
have bothered to write them? It is not generally
profitable to make people as uncomfortable as these
plays seem designed to do. . . .

Both plays, too, contain a peculiarly personal indictment of human baseness, of man's moral nature
isolated in all its unloveliness and increasingly separated from complicating political implications.[52]

Somewhat more guardedly than Wilson, H. J.
Oliver also subscribes to the idea that *Timon* is a bold
dramatic experiment. In his introduction to the new
Arden edition of *Timon* (1959), Oliver finds it unusual
that certain balances are found in the play, as prosperity
and adversity, hypocritical flattery and flattering cyn-
icism, contrasting refusals of various creditors, visits to
Timon in the woods counterpointed against each other
and against the visits paid by each group to Timon in
the beginning of the play.[53]

Whether Timon himself is regarded as a saint or a
fool by the critics who see the play as experimental, he
is invariably considered a character, half ideal, half real,
in isolation from mankind. Oliver believes that as a
tragic hero, Timon "lacks depth and profundity."
Timon is someone who isolates himself from humanity
by the expedient of avoiding the conflict.[54]

Although Oliver is aware of the intellectual texture
of the play, he differs from most other critics who see
Timon as experimental in that he does not regard the
play as an expression of Shakespeare's own mind:

Timon's misanthropy, like everything else in
Shakespeare's plays, is part of a dramatized situation
and is in no sense a lyrical statement of the poet's
own belief; and Timon's invective, for which the
play has received most of such praise as has generally

been given it, is all the more remarkable when one pauses to reflect that it states an attitude from which, through the presence of the Steward, Shakespeare has disassociated himself completely.[55]

The presence of the Steward mitigates the theme of complete despair by "refusal to believe that suffering is all."

E. A. J. Honigmann believes that Shakespeare "knew precisely where he was going" in writing *Timon*. Timon himself is designed as a character in isolation and the apartness from each other of the minor characters in the play mirror the predicament of the protagonist.[56]

The play is experimental, dealing in abstractions and generalizations.[57] The "shock tactics" of the sex theme might suggest the Inns of Court as a likely audience, for crudeness characterizes the treatment of the subject in literature designed for the Inns. Also, the great banquet in Act I and the mock banquet in Act III would lend themselves well to an evening performance at an Inn.[58]

Honigmann has high praise for the intellectual qualities of the play. He objects to Coleridge's hint that *Timon* is an "after-vibration" of *Lear*.[59] Honigmann refuses to regard *Timon* as "a left-over."[60] Rather, *Timon* should be classed with "the dark comedies" as one of Shakespeare's "probing plays" in which he found it rewarding "to ask frightening questions and close them with perfunctory answers."[61]

The fascination with the intellectual quality of the play as a reflection of Shakespeare's own mind and with the protagonist as a character in isolation is felt by at least one philosopher, Walter Kaufmann, professor of philosophy at Princeton. In *From Shakespeare to Ex-*

istentialism, Kaufmann sees Timon's isolation through the disloyalty of his friends as probably mirrored in Shakespeare's own experience. Kaufmann defends his biographical-philosophical interpretation of the character of Timon in a dialogue between "the author" and "the critic." The author asks, "Was the author of *Hamlet* and *Timon* less lonely than the writers today?" The critic replies that he was because man's inhumanity to man is now greater than ever, as symbolized by the atom bomb: "We have weapons of destruction that threaten to wipe out mankind. That creates a sense of futility." But the author observes that Shakespeare and the writers today have an equal sense of the meaninglessness of life: "The prime source of any feeling of futility, frustration, and anxiety lies in the self. . . ."[62] In *Macbeth,* Shakespeare recognized that life is "a tale told by an idiot, full of sound and fury,/Signifying nothing," and he expresses the same attitude toward life in *Timon,* thus identifying himself as an existentialist without knowing it:

> My long sickness
> Of health and living now begins to mend
> And nothing brings me all things.
> (V.i.189–191)

In discerning an existentialist attitude in Timon—that nothing is more real than nothing—Kaufmann concludes that Timon's disillusionment does not lead him beyond this world, that Timon only wants oblivion, to lie "where the light foam of the sea may beat/Thy grave-stone daily."[63]

Timon, then, reflecting Shakespeare's own experience, stands on one side of a gulf which separates him from the rest of mankind. According to Kaufmann, this gulf is bridged by an "intermediate nobility" which consists of loyalty. In *Hamlet, Lear,* and *Timon,* the "bridges" are Horatio, Kent, and Flavius, respectively. Timon and Hamlet "are the lords and owners of their faces," whereas Flavius and Horatio are "but stewards of their excellence."[64] Loyalty all should have, "and it is all-important in Shakespeare's godless world. . . . But it is a measure of Shakespeare's disillusionment that he considered it so exceedingly rare."[65] In accordance with this concept, the loyal steward, Flavius, might will be the "touchstone" character in the play rather than Apemantus, the cynic, whom most critics seem to have accepted.

In the mid-twentieth century, critics of *Timon*—Miss Ellis-Fermor, Alexander, Sisson, Collins, Maxwell, Oliver, Harold Wilson, Honigmann, and the philosopher, Kaufmann—have praised the intellectual quality of the play. This special intellectual quality has appealed to a novelist, Vladimir Nabokov, the title of whose novel, *Pale Fire* (1962), is taken from *Timon.*[66] The leading figure in the novel is a madman who thinks he is a king. In isolation from humanity, he creates his own reality in accidental combinations of disconnected and sometimes unreal thoughts. Absolute meaning is non-existent. The thesis lies rather in the lines quoted from *Timon* in a translation from a mythical language, Zemblan. These lines (IV.iii.439–445), to the effect that everything steals from everything else, are, ironically enough, adapted by Shakespeare from Anacreon, probably through Ronsard.[67] Like the king, the novel depends for its existence on a series of disconnected happenings which glance off rather than follow each other, in a manner as episodic as the happenings in the play. Like the play, too, perhaps, if more recent critics of *Timon* are correct, the novel does not contain an absolute value, a text, but merely displays an intellectual texture.

To summarize, the theorists who explained the structural peculiarities of *Timon* on the basis of divided authorship looked for all the work in the play which was inferior, and which, therefore, in their opinion, Shakespeare could not have written. In so doing, they tore the play apart. The play continued on very uncertain ground until the students of imagery began their search for patterns repeating each other throughout the play. In so doing, they concentrated on finding as much evidence as possible to support any given image pattern. This search was a positive approach to the play, in contrast to the previous negative attempt to find everything "inferior" in it. The image studies, then, served to introduce a trend of favorable criticism of *Timon*. Scholars became aware of rich meanings in the play which had been previously overlooked.

The pro-*Timon* tendency of the image studies was reinforced by the studies of scholars familiar with experimental forms of drama, the theory of relativity as applied to literature, or existentialist philosophy. The explanation of the unique nature of the play as "experimental" was to some extent, at least, another attempt to explain the structural irregularities, paralleling previous attempts of those who accounted for structural peculiarities by arguing the presence of two hands in the composition of the play, or by suggesting that Shakespeare had left the play unfinished. However, the "experimental" theory put more emphasis on meaning than did the theories of divided authorship or incompleteness. In this emphasis on "meaning," the "experimental" theorists resembled the Romantic critics, but with a difference. Whereas the Romantic critics looked for truth in the play, most of the "experimental" critics looked for intellectual texture.

From 1930 on, the period is chaotic because it still
witnesses every shade of attitude toward *Timon*, from
that in an issue of *The Saturday Review* which records
Timon as being "by Shakespeare *et al.*"—to that which
regards Shakespeare as emotionally disturbed when he
wrote the play (Hardin Craig)—to the idea that *Timon*
is a rough draft showing "Shakespeare at work" (Oliver)—to the idea that *Timon* is a very great play indeed
(Collins, Harold Wilson, Honigmann). The question-
ing of values has worked in favor of *Timon's* acceptance.
Arguing against permitting "academic moralists" to
apply their "homemade foot-rules" to drama, Angus
Wilson summarizes the attitude with which several recent critics approach their criticism of *Timon:*

> It is surely neither romantic nor irresponsible to
> refuse to care whether the moral force of "Timon"
> or of "Pericles" or of "The Way of the World" be
> mature and healthy or not. Shakespeare's most ma-
> ture work, "The Tempest," ends in despair: it is cer-
> tainly not a tonic for a sick society.[68]

FOOTNOTES

1. J. M. Robertson, *Shakespeare and Chapman* (London,
1917), pp. 133–134.
2. H. Dugdale Sykes, *Sidelights on Elizabethan Drama* (Oxford, 1924), p. 48.
3. Robert Gould, *The Play-House, a Satyr. Writ in the Year*
1685. [In *Poems Chiefly Consisting of Satyrs and Satyrical Epistles*
(London, 1689).]
4. *The Works of William Shakespear*, ed. William Warburton (London, 1747), VI. See particularly his comment on "no
levell'd malice" (p. 150) and "Dry up thy marrows" (p. 213).
5. Warburton (London, 1847), *op cit.*, VI, 150.
6. F. P. Wilson, "Shakespeare and the Diction of Common
Life," *Proceedings, Br. Acad.* (London, 1944), XXVII, 167–197.
7. *Ibid.*
8. Caroline Spurgeon, *Shakespeare's Imagery and What It
Tells Us* (Cambridge, Eng., 1935), 198–199.
9. *Ibid.*, p. 343–344.

10. Una Ellis-Fermor, *Some Recent Research in Shakespeare's Imagery*. Shakespeare Assn. Papers (London, 1937), p. 27.

11. Wolfgang Clemen, *The Development of Shakespeare's Imagery* (New York, 1961). (Revised English edition, Cambridge, Mass., 1951, based on *Shakespeare's Bilder* [Bonn, 1936]).

12. *Ibid.*, p. 176.

13. J. W. Draper, "The Theme of *Timon of Athens*," *MLR* (1934), XXIX, 20–31.

14. *Ibid.*, p. 22.

15. *Ibid.*

16. Una Ellis-Fermor, *The Frontiers of Drama* (New York, 1946), p. 81.

17. *Ibid.*, p. 74.

18. R. P. Draper, "*Timon of Athens*," *SQ* (1957), VIII, 195–200.

19. William Empson, *The Structure of Complex Words* (London, 1951), Chapter VIII, "Timon's Dog," pp. 175–184.

20. John Holloway, *The Story of the Night* (London, 1961), pp. 131–133.

21. Irving Ribner, *Patterns in Shakespearian Tragedy* (New York, 1960), pp. 140–156.

22. Willard Farnham, *Shakespeare's Tragic Frontier: The World of His Final Tragedies* (Berkeley and Los Angeles, 1950), pp. 39–77.

23. *Ibid.*, p. 68.

24. *Ibid.*, pp. 69–71.

25. *The Pictorial Edition of the Works of Shakspere*, ed. Charles Knight (London, 1839), V, 337.

26. Una Ellis-Fermor, *The Jacobean Drama: An Interpretation* (London, 1936), p. 259–264.

27. *Ibid.*, pp. 265–266.

28. *Ibid.*, p. 266.

29. *Ibid.*, p. 265.

30. *Ibid.*

31. Peter Alexander, *Shakespeare's Life and Art* (New York, 1961), pp. 182–188 (first edition, 1939).

32. *Ibid.*, p. 185.

33. *Ibid.*, p. 186.

34. Ellis-Fermor (London, 1936), *op. cit.*, p. 33–34.

35. A. S. Collins, "*Timon of Athens:* A Reconsideration," *RES* (April, 1946), XXII, 96–108.

36. *Ibid.*, p. 97.

37. *Ibid.*, p. 108.

38. *Ibid.*, p. 96.

39. *Ibid.*, p. 104.

40. *Ibid.*, p. 108.

41. Henri Fluchère, *Shakespeare*, trans. by Guy Hamilton (London, 1953), p. 257.
42. *Ibid.*
43. *Ibid.*
44. *Ibid.*
45. *William Shakespeare The Complete Works*, ed. Charles Jasper Sisson (London, 1954), p. 910.
46. *Ibid.*, p. xv.
47. *Ibid.*, p. 910.
48. *Ibid.*
49. *Ibid.*
50. Harold S. Wilson, *On the Design of Shakespearian Tragedy* (Toronto, 1957), pp. 145, 156.
51. *Ibid.*, pp. 154–155.
52. *Ibid.*
53. *Timon of Athens*, Arden edition. ed. H. J. Oliver (London, 1959), pp. xlviii–xlix.
54. *Ibid.*, p. 1.
55. *Ibid.*, p. li.
56. E. A. J. Honigmann, *"Timon of Athens,"* SQ (1961), XII, 15.
57. *Ibid.*, p. 17.
58. *Ibid.*, pp. 17–18.
59. *Ibid.*, p. 20.
60. *Ibid.*
61. *Ibid.*, p. 17.
62. Walter Kaufmann, *From Shakespeare to Existentialism* (New York, 1960), p. 28.
63. *Ibid.*, p. 13.
64. *Ibid.*, p. 44.
65. *Ibid.*
66. Vladimir Nabokov, *Pale Fire* (New York, 1962), p. 42.
67. "An Essay on the Learning of Shakespeare," in *The Plays of William Shakespeare*, ed. Richard Farmer (London, 1800), I. xciii.
68. Angus Wilson, "Fashions in Criticisms . . .," *New York Times Book Review Section* (July 2, 1961), p. 12.

Part Three
TIMON AS A STAGE PLAY

VIII

AN EMPTY COFFER: *Structure and Meaning to the Audience*

Pass by and curse thy fill, but pass. (V.iv)

TIMON OF ATHENS has been performed many times but it has not been a success on the stage in its original form. Thomas Shadwell's version of the play was successful when performed during the late seventeenth and early eighteenth centuries. Some academic performances have been pronounced good. With these exceptions, people have not been interested in seeing the play. Professional performances have not had long runs.

Performances of special interest have been those in Thomas Shadwell's version, Richard Cumberland's version, George Lamb's version, and performances—as Shakespeare wrote the play—at the Old Vic, in Paul Heyse's translation in German at Munich in 1910, and in Daniel Auer's translation in French at Geneva in 1950.

The first known staging of *Timon* was in the version of Thomas Shadwell in 1678.[1] This version is important because, as will be seen, the criticism of Shake-

speare's *Timon* in the late seventeenth century by
Gerard Langbaine and by Charles Gildon was based on
Shadwell's version; Shadwell's version or its offshoots
was the only *Timon* produced for eighteenth-century
audiences; Southey, among the Romantics, thought it
sufficiently important to condemn; and the proponents
of divided authorship cited Shadwell's changes in support of their theory of the inadequacies of the play as a
work wholly by Shakespeare.

Langbaine's brief reference to *Timon* appears under "Shadwell" in Langbaine's *An Account of the English Dramatick Poets*.[2] Langbaine merely writes that
"The Play is originally Shakespeare's; but so imperfectly printed, that 'tis not divided into Acts," and
that he has not time to inquire into how much Shadwell "has added or expung'd."[3] Since elsewhere, Langbaine admits his admiration for Shadwell's work,[4] it
would seem fairly safe to assume that had he had time
to review Shadwell's version of *Timon*, his review
would have been favorable.

Charles Gildon was not so pleased as Langbaine with
Shadwell's version. Of Shadwell's characterization of
the Poet in *Timon*, Gildon writes:

> Mr *Shadwell* who has pretended to alter this Play
> has made him a very Scoundrel, and the Players
> always take Care in Dress and Action to make him
> more so.
> But this is not the only thing in which Mr *Shad-
> well* has made this Poem worse in the Copy or Amend-
> ments, than it is in the Original; He has created two
> Ladies of his own very odd Design.[5]

Since Shadwell's is the only version of *Timon* known
to have been produced in the late seventeenth century,
Robert Gould undoubtedly refers—disparagingly—to
Shadwell's version in the following lines:

In *Timon, Lear, The Tempest,* we may find
Vast Images of thy unbounded mind;
These have been alter'd by our *Poets* now,
And with success too, that we must allow,
Third days they get when part of *thee* is shown,
Which they but seldom do when *all's* their own.[6]

Shadwell's version had a number of revivals between its first production in 1678 and its last in 1745, after which it still lived on in the revisions of James Love (1768), Richard Cumberland (1771), and Thomas Hull (1786). Of these, none was a stage success, but Cumberland's is of some interest because it was produced by Garrick. Shadwell's alone received critical attention over a long period of time.

During the Romantic period, Robert Southey gave *Timon* as an example of the attempt of some neoclassical playwrights to "improve" Shakespeare: "men who, when they committed the sacrilege could not be conscious that it was sacrilege they were committing."[7] Southey exploded as follows about Shadwell's *Timon:*

> Shadwell boasted that he had made 'Timon of Athens' into a play. The execution was worthy of the attempt and the attempt was worthy of Shadwell, whose bust in Westminster Abbey ought to have been cast either in lead or in brass, or in an emblematic amalgam of the two metals. . . . Shadwell could not degrade himself, for nothing could degrade him.[8]

Several proponents of the theory that *Timon* showed the presence "of two or more hands" recalled Shadwell's statement about *Timon*—that he had "made it into a Play"—and used it to support their view of the general inferiority of *Timon* as a work wholly by Shakespeare. Thomas Marc Parrott, for instance, introduced his monograph, in which Chapman is proposed as the

second author, with the following reference to Shadwell's version:

> Shadwell, the Restoration playwright, was no idle
> boaster when he affirmed in the dedication to his
> version of *Timon* 'the inimitable hand of Shakespeare
> never made more masterly strokes than in this work,
> yet I can truly say I have made it into a play.' And
> so he did. To the lover of Shakespeare, Shadwell's
> version, with its fickle hero wavering like the ass of
> Buridan between a constant mistress and a heartless
> bride, and its alternating scenes of Restoration flip-
> pancy and Restoration rant, reads like a profanation.
> But Shadwell's version held the stage for over half a
> century, and all attempts to revive the old play have
> been signal failures. The explanation of the dramatic
> impossibility of *Timon* is after all, quite simple. There
> is not enough of the creative power of Shakespeare in
> the play to quicken the whole into dramatic life.[9]

In order to produce a successful version, Shadwell
made basic changes in the structure of *Timon*. In these
changes, Shadwell put his finger unerringly on certain
portions of the play, the coherence of which is still in
question. Critics who believe that a play should have
an ordered interconnection of scenes are likely to agree
with Shadwell's well-known dedication of his *Timon* to
George, Duke of Buckingham—that although originally
written by Shakespeare, Shadwell "made it into a
Play."[10]

In his Act I, Shadwell omits the foreshadowing of
the action of the play from the Poet-Painter dialogue
which opens Shakespeare's *Timon*.[11] His purpose, still
considered valid by some critics of dramaturgy, is to
cut any dialogue which might destroy the element of
suspense. Shadwell also delays the first banquet scene
from its position in Shakespeare's *Timon* near the be-

ginning of the play (I.ii) to Act II. Apparently, he desires to use the banquet scene as the exciting force in the rising action of the play, rather than as part of the exposition of Timon's situation.

An important change which he makes in the banquet scene would bear out this intention. In Shadwell's Act II, Alcibiades is not present at Timon's first banquet, as he is in Shakespeare's play (I.ii). Instead, Timon petitions the Senators to readmit the exiled Alcibiades to Athens. Not only does Shadwell's change contribute action to the scene, but by indicating early in the play that Timon takes an interest in the career of Alcibiades, Shadwell has attempted to create a closer link between the Alcibiades subplot and the main plot. This structural change is particularly interesting because, as has been seen in the history of the structural criticism of *Timon,* critics have long debated whether the sub- and main plots are well knit, and have drawn deductions therefrom about the literary merit and even the authorship of the play.[12] Considerable critical comment has also been evoked by Shakespeare's burlesque scene (II.ii) between Apemantus and the Fool and the Page. The scene has been thought to indicate corruption,[13] divided authorship,[14] or the unfinished state of the text.[15] Shadwell omits this scene.

In Shakespeare's *Timon,* the turning point of the action in the subplot, the exile of Alcibiades, occurs in Act III immediately after the turning point of the action in the main plot, the lines in which Timon despatches his Steward to invite Timon's false friends to a second banquet (III.iv), at which Timon will hurl hot water in their faces. Shadwell delays the scene in which Alcibiades is exiled until after Timon's banquet and Timon's departure from Athens. In Shadwell's version, the exile of Alcibiades thus occurs in Act IV, and serves as the tragic force in the falling action of the play. Also in Act IV, Shadwell omits the visit of the thieves to Timon in the woods, an interesting omission since in Shakespeare's *Timon* (IV.iii), this scene has been criticized by later editors as either irrelevant or out-of-place in the development of the plot.

In Shakespeare's Act V, the brief scene in which a Soldier happens upon Timon's grave and takes a wax imprint of the epitaph to give to Alcibiades (V.iii) has been considered awkward by many editors since Pope.[16] Shadwell omits this scene, and simply has a Messenger bring word to Alcibiades of Timon's death.

Not only does Shadwell change the structure of the play but he also changes the meaning, toward which he takes a cynical view: (1) He gives Timon not one tragic flaw but three—his Timon retains the flaw of irrational liberality and adds those of concupiscence and ingratitude; (2) He reduces the stature of Timon by depriving him of the strong loyalty of his servants; (3) He makes the play the vehicle for the expression of trivial sentiments, probably intended as satire on the contemporary scene—satire of heroic verse, coquettes, and Tories.

Why did Shadwell enlarge on Timon's flaws? Perhaps he wanted poetic justice *à la* Rymer and Dennis: a man must be bad indeed to fall so low. Timon's sexual lust is revealed in the complaints of his mistress, Evandra, a character whom Shadwell adds to the play. For instance:

> The only treasures a poor Maid possest,
> I sacrificed to you, and rather chose
> To throw my self away, than you shou'd be
> Uneasie in your wishes.

In reply, Timon reasons that "Man is not master of his appetites" (Act I). Timon is also guilty of ingratitude in his relations with Evandra. He has reduced her to lamenting, "I trusted to your honour, and lost mine" (Act I) before he finally concedes, "I've been ungrateful to her, why should I/Blame Villains who are so to me?" (Act III).

In Shakespeare's *Timon,* the loyalty of Timon's servants mirrored favorably their master's character. The touching devotion to Timon exhibited in the scene in which the three servants leave their master's household (IV.ii) was commended by critics as early as Pope (through his selection of the scene as one of the "beauties" in the play).[17] In his edition of *Timon,* in Shakespeare's *Works,* Johnson noted:

> Nothing contributes more to the exaltation of Timon's character than the zeal and fidelity of his servants. Nothing but real virtue can be honoured by domesticks; nothing but impartial kindness can gain affection from dependants.[19]

Shadwell cuts this "servant" scene.

In fact, Shadwell goes further than omitting passages depicting the loyalty of Timon's servants. He makes Timon's Steward as disloyal as Timon's false friends. In the opening lines of the play in Shadwell's version (Act I), Shadwell's Steward exclaims:

> What vast rewards to nauseous Flatterers,
> To Pimps, and Women, what Estates he gives!
> And shall I have no share? Be gon, all Honesty,
> Thou foolish, slender, thredbare, starving thing,
>   be gon!

No lines parallel to these occur in Shakespeare's *Timon.* Farther along, however, parallel lines occur which clearly illustrate the difference between Shakespeare's and Shadwell's treatment of the Steward. In an aside

(I.ii), Shakespeare's Steward expresses pity for Timon's plight:

> Well, would I were
> Gently put out of Office, before I were forc'd out;
> Happier is he that has no friend to feede,
> Then such that do e'ne Enemies exceede.
> I bleed inwardly for my Lord.
>
> *(Exit)*

But Shadwell's Steward (Act II) has a selfish and a contemptuous attitude toward his master:

> Would I were gently turn'd
> Out of my Office; lest he shou'd borrow all
> I have gotten in his service. Well!
> *Happier is he that has no friend to feed,*
> *Than such who do ev'n Enemies exceed.*
>
> *(Exit)*

The difference between Shadwell's and Shakespeare's treatment of the Steward is again exemplified in the visits to Timon in the woods. In Shadwell's version, Evandra, not the Steward, visits Timon. On the occasion of this meeting, cynical lines given by Shakespeare to Apemantus: "That the bleake ayre . . . Cawdle thy Morning taste" (IV.iii.222–226) are transferred by Shadwell to Timon: "Is not the bleak Air . . . Caudle to thee?" (Act IV). Finally, in place of Timon's lines to the Steward (IV.iii.503–504), "You perpetuall sober Gods. I do proclaime/One honest man," Shadwell substitutes the following lines addressed by Timon to Evandra (Act IV): "I now pronounce to all the world, there is/One woman honest."

Shadwell's *Timon* is no "powerful lesson against ostentatious liberality," as Johnson later wrote of Shakespeare's play. Conveying, if it conveys anything, the not-very-original message that we are all human, Shadwell's *Timon* was less instructive but undoubtedly more pleasing to audiences in London, who expected, in "a domestick Tragedy," a less lofty tone than Shakespeare's. Most theatergoers could probably identify themselves more easily with Shadwell's lustful Timon than with Shakespeare's misogynic as well as misanthropic Timon.

No doubt audiences were diverted by the trivia which Shadwell added to the play—the jests at heroic poetry, silly, flirtatious belles, and corrupt politicians. Satire of heroic poetry occurs in Shadwell's Acts I and II. In Act I, Demetrius, Timon's Steward, converses with the Poet on heroic verse:

> *Dem.* What d'ye mean by style? that of good sence is all alike; that is to say, with apt and easie words, not one too little or too much: And this I think good style.
> *Poet.* O Sir, you are wide o'th' matter! apt and easie!
> Heroiks must be lofty and high sounding;
> No easie Language in Heroick Verse;
> 'Tis most unfit: for should I name a Lion,
> I must not in Heroicks call him so!
> *Dem.* What then?
> *Poet.* I'de as soon call him an Ass. No thus—
> The fierce *Numidian* Monarch of the Beasts.
> *Dem.* That's lofty, is it?
> *Poet.* O yes! but a Lion would sound so badly, not to be Endur'd, and a Bull too—but
> The mighty Warriour of the horned Race:
> Ah—how that sounds!
> *Dem.* Then I perceive sound's the great matter in this way.
> *Poet.* Ever while you live.
> *Dem.* How would you sound a Fox as you call it?
> *Poet.* A Fox is but a scurvey Beast for Heroick Verse.
> *Dem.* Hum—is it so? how will a Raven do in Heroick?
> *Poet.* Oh very well, Sir.

That black and dreadful fate-denouncing fowl.
Dem. An excellent sound—But let me see your Piece.
Poet. I'le read it—'Tis a good morrow to the Lord
Timon.
Dem. Do you make good morrow sound loftily?
Poet. Oh very loftily!—
　　　The fringed Vallance of your eyes advance,
　　　Shake off your Canopy'd and downie trance;
　　　Phoebus *already quaffs the morning dew,*
　　　Each does his daily lease of life renew.

And so on. In Act II, Apemantus, the cynic, rails at the
Poet's conception of verse:

Apem. Thy Poetrie's insipid, none can taste it:
Thou art a wordy foolish Scribler, who
Writ'st nothing but high-sounding frothy stuff;
Thou spread'st, and beat'st out thy poor little sence,
'Tis all leaf-gold, it has no weight in it.
Thou lov'st impertinent description,
And when thou hast a rapture, it is not
The sacred rapture of a Poet, but
Incoherent, extravagant, and unnatural,
Like mad-mens thoughts, and this thou call'st Poetical.
Poet. You are judge! shall dull Philosophers judge
Of us the nimble fancies, and quick spirits
Of the Age?
Apem. The Cox-combs of the Age:
Are there such eminent fopperies as in the
Poets of this time? their most unreasonable heads
Are whimsical, and fantastick as Fidlers,
They are the scorn and laughter of all witty men,
The folly of you makes the Art contemptible,
None of you have the judgement of a Gander.
Poet. You are a base snarling Critick; write your
Self, do and you dare.

Since Shadwell's *Timon* is dedicated to George Villiers, Duke of Buckingham, who seven years earlier, in

1671, brought forth *The Rehearsal,* in which Dryden's heroic verse is satirized, Dryden is certainly a possible target for Shadwell. Dryden's *Macflecknoe,* satirizing Shadwell, may have been circulated as early as 1678.[19] In any case, Shadwell's satire of heroic poetry is an interpolation which gives his version of *Timon* a lighter tone than that in Shakespeare's play.

Besides the satire of heroic verse, Shadwell satirizes the coquette of his period. His observations, like his jabs at heroic verse, are not original. In character, they resemble those expressed more succinctly by Pope later in *The Rape of the Lock.* Shadwell's Melissa, a titled beauty who demands marriage, is introduced at her dressing table in lines the silliness of which forecasts Belinda in Pope's *Rape.* For instance:

> *Mel.*   I love
> To make those Fellows die for me, and I
> All the while look so scornfully, and then with my
> Head on one side, with a languishing eye I do so
> Kill 'em again: Prithee, what do they say of me,
> *Chloe?*
> *Chloe.* Say! That you are the Queen of all their hearts,
> Their Goddess, their Destiny, and talk of *Cupids*
>   flames.

*   *   *

> *Mel.* I have been too long this morning in dressing.
> *Chloe.* Oh no, I vow you have been but bare three
>   hours.
>   (Act II)

These lines and others of the same tenor, "This pretty curle/Does give you such a killing Grace" (Act II), " 'Tis our interest to be honest" (Act II), "I look so pretty to day, I could/Kiss my self" (Act II), are Shad-

well's way of breaking up the great blocks of Shakespeare's central themes of love, ingratitude, and hate.
Since Shadwell was a follower of Shaftesbury,[20] and after *Timon,* wrote two political comedies,[21] *The Lancashire Witches* (1681), and *The Amorous Bigotte* (1690), a possibility exists that certain vituperative statements about politics which Shadwell added to the play had some bearing on the contemporary political situation in London. In fact, the instructive nature of the political satire in Shadwell's *Timon* is specifically commended by "I. H." some years later in "The Stage Vindicated: A Satyr." Part of the reference to Shadwell's *Timon* reads:

> Can you in K——gs empty Lessons find,
> Such moving truths to work upon the Mind.
> The Libertine who burns with lawless Fires,
> Sinks in the Scene, and in blue Flames expires.
> How oft has Vice been follow'd to the throne,
> And tyrant Kings in bloody Colours shown.[22]

Some of Shadwell's lines may have a contemporary political import because they do not appear to advance the plot or develop characterization, but merely to perform the static function of padding the parts. Since Timon has been made a libertine as well as a spendthrift in Shadwell's play, he may conceivably represent the known qualities of Charles II, but the satire of corruption is general, and could be applicable to any period to some leading politician or other. Apemantus is the most frequent mouthpiece for these added lines. For example, in Act I:

> What should Great Men be proud of stead of noise
> And pomp and show, and holding up their heads,
> And cocking of their noses; pleas'd to see

> Base smiling Knaves, and cringing fools bow to 'em?
> Did they but see their own ridiculous folly,
> Their mean and absurd vanities; they'd hide
> Their heads within some dark and little corner,
> And be afraid that every fool should find 'em.

When the Poet urges Timon to send Apemantus "to the Areopagus" (Cavalier Parliament?)[23] so that he will be punished, Apemantus replies,

> Thus innocence, truth and merit often suffer.
> Whil'st injurers, oppressors and desertless fools
> Swell in their brief authority, look big
> And strut in Furs; 'tis a foul shame,
> But 'tis a loathsome Age,—it has been long
> Imposthumating with its villanie;
> And now the swelling's broken out
> In most contagious ulcers; no place free
> From the destructive Pestilence of manners;
> Out upon't, 'tis time the world should end!
>
> (Act I)

Shadwell transfers to Apemantus, with certain changes, the following lines of the loyal Steward in Shakespeare's *Timon:*

> So the Gods blesse me,
> When all our Offices have beene opprest
> With riotous Feeders, when our Vaults have wept
> With drunken spilth of Wine; when every roome
> Hath blaz'd with Lights, and braid with Minstrelsie,
> I have retyr'd me to a wastefull cocke,
> And set mine eyes at flow.
>
> (II.ii.176–182)

In Shadwell's version, the above passage, spoken by Apemantus rather than the Steward, appears as follows:

> So the gods bless me.
> When all your Offices have been opprest

With riotous feeders, when every Vault has wept
With drunken spilth of wine, when every room
Has blaz'd with lights, and bray'd with Minstrels,
Or roaring singing drunkards; I have retir'd
To my poor homely Cell, and set my eyes
At flow for thee, because I find something in
Thee that might be worthy—but as thou art I
Hate and scorn thee.

                                        (Act II)

No purpose seems to be accomplished in transferring the above lines from the loyal Steward to Apemantus and in adding the final expression of "hate and scorn" except to emphasize further the denunciation of Timon. Later in Act III, Apemantus, in Timon's presence, jibes at government:

The Government's to blame in suffering the things
    I rail at.
In suffering Judges without Beards, or Law, Secretaries that
Can't write;
Generals that durst not fight, Ambassadors that can't
    speak sence;
Block-heads to be great Ministers, and Lord it over
    witty men;
Suffering great men to sell their Country for filthy
    bribes,
Old limping Senators to sell their Souls
For vile extortion: Matrons to turn incontinent;
And Magistrates to pimp for their own Daughters.

Why Shadwell saw fit to add these sentiments to Shakespeare's play can only be conjectured. In line with his known political attitudes, and his production of avowedly "political" plays, certainly there is some basis for the assumption that the observations are meant to be contemporary allusions to the government of

Charles. Whether they are or are not, however, is of little import in the weighing of the changes as criticism of Shakespeare's play. For whatever reason, Shadwell evidently believed that *Timon* in its original form was a little flat, that it needed not only structural changes but also spice added to the content.

In summary, while making changes in the structure which may well be considered sound dramaturgy from the neoclassical point of view, Shadwell is not concerned with possible deeper meanings of the play. Rather, his objectives seem to be: making the play more of a domestic tragedy (by reducing Timon from an ideal figure to an ordinary man); spicing the play with light contemporary satire of women (through the added character of Melissa); making thrusts at heroic poetry (through his extensive additions to the lines of the Steward); and indulging in political criticism (through the jibes at corruption which he adds to Shakespeare's characterization of Apemantus).

While Shadwell's version of *Timon* was still being revived occasionally, a comic Timon play, Lucianic in source, appeared briefly at Drury Lane Theatre. Written by John Kelly and produced in 1733, this version, entitled *Timon in Love*,[24] was almost a literal translation of a French play based on Lucian by Delisle de la Drévetière.[25] The French version had "Brought Paris seventy crowded Nights together,"[26] but the English translation, even with seventeen added English "airs,"[27] did not run more than a few times. Although critics sometimes refer to these plays (apparently without having read them) as if a relationship might exist between them and Shakespeare's *Timon*, no evidence has been produced to indicate any relationship whatsoever between these plays and Shakespeare's.[28]

During the eighteenth century, Shadwell's *Timon*

was adapted by three dramatists, James Love (James Dance), Richard Cumberland, and Thomas Hull. Love's version, acted at Richmond ten times during 1768, and not produced thereafter, is an embarrassing example of the intrusion of sentiment into late eighteenth-century drama.[29] Since Love's is basically Shadwell's *Timon*, it does not deserve separate treatment except for noting that Love felt it necessary to add sentiment in order to make the play acceptable to his audience. As actual criticism of *Timon* as a work of art, Love's changes play the same role as does the "modernizing" of a Greek drama. That is, the changes do not affect the critical evaluation of the original play. The sentimental overtones which Love adds to the play are well illustrated by the final speech of Alcibiades:

> Unhappy Timon!—bounteous to excess!
> Who cou'd have thought thy virtues strain'd to th'
>   height,
> Shou'd be the cause of thy disastrous fate,
> And stamp a living satire on mankind.[30]

Love, an actor as well as a writer, played Apemantus.

Thomas Hull's version of Shadwell was produced at Covent Garden, May 13, 1786, but was not heard of again.[31] Richard Cumberland's version created more interest because he was a better-known playwright, and because the version was produced by Garrick. Of special note are the letters exchanged by David Garrick and Cumberland about the play. These letters reveal the respect Garrick had for Shakespeare's version and for the critical standards of eighteenth-century audiences, and the contempt Cumberland had for the critical standards of these same audiences, the low tastes of which, he felt, made his adaptation necessary. Correspondence between Garrick and Cumberland with reference to *Timon* began on January 25, 1768, when Cumberland wrote Garrick:

> Sir, I beg leave to enclose an altered copy of Shakespeare's *Timon,* with the addition of a new character, which I dare say you will be polite enough to read. . . .[32]

Cumberland went on to say that Coleman had already rejected the play, but that Cumberland hoped Garrick would read it. Garrick did so, and on February 5, 1769, replied:

> I have read "Timon" over very carefully, and think that the alterations have great merit in the writing part, but as they do not add greatly to the pathos of the play, and break into its simplicity, I really believe that the lovers of Shakespeare would condemn us for not giving them "Timon" as it stands in the original. I think that excellent rule for writing as it is laid down by Horace, *simplex et unum,* was never more verified than in Shakespeare's "Timon." I could have wished that the same hand which has altered "Timon" had been employed upon a less meritorious play.[33]

Garrick's praise of Timon's "unity"—apparently a combined unity of structure and meaning, for he speaks of the play's "pathos" and breaking into "its simplicity"—has never been emphasized by critics, for some reason. Even as a classical play, Garrick could scarcely give it higher praise than to write, as he does above, that the "excellent rule for writing as it is laid down by Horace, *simplex et unum,* was never more verified than in Shakespeare's 'Timon.' " To this praise of Shakespeare's *Timon* and detraction of his own version,

Cumberland on February 7 makes the following cynical
reply:

> I give you many thanks for the trouble you have
> taken in the perusal of "Timon" and your speedy re-
> turn of it. I shall be glad to see the time when sim-
> plicity is a recommendation to any dramatic piece.
> It was in conformity to the depravity of modern taste
> that I altered Shakespeare; and conceived that, when
> I robbed him of the beauties of his native simplicity,
> I made him less venerable indeed, but more suitably
> equipped for the company he was to keep.[34]

Cumberland, that is, does not quarrel with Garrick's
praise of the "simplicity" of *Timon,* but justifies his
own adaptation on the basis of the "depravity" of the
taste of audiences. No further correspondence on the
subject occurred until the early fall of 1771, when
Cumberland reminded Garrick of his "half-begotten
brat, called *Timon.*" Shortly thereafter, Cumberland
wrote Garrick, "You make me very happy to receive
your appreciation [of Timon]."

After two months of rehearsal, the play was performed first on December 4, 1771.[35] One critic, Arthur
Murphy, found Cumberland's alterations "bad."[36]
Another, Thomas Davies, wrote that Cumberland "de-
stroyed all pity for the principal character of the
play. . . . It is indeed a miserable alteration of one of
Shakespeare's noblest productions."[37] The play was
presented eleven times in 1771 and 1772, with one re-
vival in 1783.[38]

Cumberland's version of *Timon* is even more sentimental than Love's. Cumberland retains the mistress
given to Timon by Shadwell, and also gives Timon a
daughter, Evanthe, with whom Alcibiades falls in love.
How this added stimulus evokes sentiment is illustrated

in the final speech of Alcibiades (corresponding to that quoted from Love's version, above):

Ah turn, *Evanthe*.
Turn from that mournful sight and look upon me;
Damp not the blessing which his dying breath
Pronounc'd upon us, and lament not him,
Who, freed from this bad world rests from his cares.
Now let us bear him to the neighboring beach,
And with such rites as soldiers use, inter him
Under the vaulted cliff (such was his will)
Strong in extremes from love to hatred tost,
In the fierce conflicts he was whelm'd and lost.[39]

This final speech of Alcibiades precedes another touching speech uttered by the dying Timon to his daughter and future son-in-law, in which Timon is unveiled as no misanthrope after all, but as a sweet old man whose gruff exterior covers a doting father. We have now moved far from any meanings in Shakespeare's play.

In view of the admiration of the Romantics for Shakespeare, it was almost inevitable that Shakespeare's own play would be given prominence during the Romantic period. Shakespeare's *Timon,* bowdlerized in conformity to "the refinement of manners," was produced at the Drury Lane in 1816, in the version of George Lamb and with Edmund Kean (whose favorite play it was) in the title role.[40] A rather full knowledge of this production is preserved in Leigh Hunt's criticism in the *Examiner.*[41]

About the merits of *Timon* as a stage play, Hunt had mixed feelings. He believed that *Timon* did not have motivation, a plot in which the culmination arises naturally and inevitably out of what precedes it; but he did think the play had deep meaning. However, he felt that George Lamb had bowdlerized the play to such an extent—tempered Timon's bitter invective, particularly that related to sex in the scene with Alcibiades and the prostitutes—that the meaning of the play was impaired. Hunt, that is, damned the structure but praised the sense.

As to structure, Hunt sees the play as a closet drama (probably much like those of his Romantic confreres): "The reader is still delighted, but he would be still more so in his closet." Hunt believes that "The moral, though strong, is obvious, and in fact, too easily anticipated; and when Timon has once fallen from his fortunes, there is little to excite further attention in the spectator."[42] In Hunt's criticism of the meaning of the play through the character of Timon, we see the contrast between the classical view of Timon's character and the Romantic view. To Johnson, Timon is "an imitation" of ostentatious liberality designed to instruct the playgoer. To Hunt, Timon is a study of idealism, a study with which the Romantic writers particularly were preoccupied. In fact, Hunt directly refutes Johnson's view of the character of Timon:

> Dr. Johnson says that the play affords 'a very powerful warning against that ostentatious liberality, which scatters bounty, but confers no benefits and buys flattery, but not friendship.' The opinion here given by Dr. Johnson is a mere dove-tailing of words, or to speak after his own fashion, a smooth adjustment of alliterative antithesis. Timon, in the midst of his squandering, does confer benefits, as in the cases of the man whom he saves from prison, and the servant whom he enables to marry. The Professor is apparently more to the purpose; but we may here remark that it is a much safer way in morals to shew the probable unhappiness that attends a doubtful virtue than to set about proving its selfishness; for by the same process, the tables may be turned on virtues the most securely reckoned upon; and the kindest

man upon earth be startled to learn that he saves others from pain, only to relieve himself.[43]

Hunt then gives his own interpretation of the meaning of Timon's plight:

> The moral of his tragedy is, not that he conferred bounties only and no benefits, nor that he mistook the love of distinction for generosity, but that human nature will allow of no excess; and that if we set out in this world with animal spirits which lead us to think too highly of it, we shall be disappointed. Shakespeare never wrote commonplace morals. . . . If Timon had been only ostentation, he would hardly have been so willing to borrow, and to think all his friends as generous as himself: he would have run mad for pride; whereas his misanthropy is really owing as in almost all instances, to an unexpected and extreme conviction of the hollowness of the human heart.[44]

That "human nature will allow of no excess"—Hunt's interpretation of the theme of *Timon*—coincides with that of Ulrici, Hazlitt, and other Romantics who see Timon as a study of idealism, or, in terms of Kantian philosophy, as a study of a man who refuses to take into account the limitations of matter in the laws of nature.

Beginning with the Romantic period, the Germans showed the most interest in the dramatic possibilities of *Timon*. The first attempt to adapt *Timon* to the German stage was that of F. J. Fischer at Prague in 1778 in Wieland's translation.[45] The production was not a success, perhaps partially because of difficulties in the translation, which contained such *faux pas* as "lap dogs" for "Dogges, and lap" (III.vi.94). Fischer's adaptation of the play included numerous cuts, one of them being "the most effective scene of the whole piece," the

banquet scene.[46] Although Schiller died before he
could produce *Timon,* he was ecstatic about its stage
possibilities, even in the production he saw in Wieland's
poor translation:

> Our stage has just accomplished a great conquest,
> the success of which will speak for itself. Shakespeare's
> *Timon of Athens* has as far as I can remember not
> appeared on any German stage. . . . I certainly do
> not know one piece in the whole of Shakespeare where
> he might stand before me more truly. No piece is
> closer to my heart, nor in any did I learn more of the
> wisdom of life than from *Timon of Athens.*[47]

Of later adaptations of Dalberg, Wehl, Lindner,
and Fresenius, only Lindner's, which was influenced by
Cumberland's, is reputed to have had some success on
the stage.[48] None of the three versions was strictly
Shakespeare's, but was patched and padded, especially
in relation to the Senate scene, which was believed to
be almost unrelated to the main plot. (It will be recalled that literary critics beginning as early as Charles
Gildon had questioned the coherence of this scene
(III.v), and its incoherence was used as evidence of
divided authorship by those who saw two or more hands
in the play.)

Wehl, the most conservative of the three patchers,
used a startling device to tie the scene more closely to
the play: He had Timon arrested by the Senate for his
behavior at the banquet. Thus dragged forcibly to the
Senate House (and into the subplot), Timon was in-
formed he had been arrested on the grounds that it is
illegal to throw boiling water and stones at people!
Conversely, the protagonist of the subplot also enters
the main plot: Alcibiades attempts to negotiate a loan
for Timon.[49]

Although in the late nineteenth century, several

minor productions of *Timon* took place in Germany, the play was so far from fulfilling Schiller's high hopes for it that August Fresenius, writing of "Timon auf der Bühne" in *Shakespeare Jahrbuch* (1895), called it "Aschenbrodeln" ("ashes soup"). A proponent of the theory of divided authorship of the play, Fresenius saw the chief task of the producer to be the reduction of the weak, "non-Shakespearean" portions to a minimum. If the producer must "cut into the flesh" in so doing, he deserves praise.[50] The divided-authorship theory, as we saw in Chapter II, grew out of attempts to explain the lack of coherence of the play. Fresenius, who had produced *Timon* unsuccessfully in the traditional way, was convinced that it could not be successfully staged.

Timon is reported to have been successfully produced in 1910 in the new Court Theatre in Munich.[51] No attempt was made to "patch up" the original with ideas from Shadwell, Cumberland, or Lamb, or to cut weak spots, or to add new material. The play was presented by the eminent poet-producer Paul Heyse, in his own translation, exactly as Shakespeare wrote it. Some scenes, such as the meeting of Timon and the Steward (III.v) were presented in front of the curtain. Raising the curtain disclosed the Senate seated behind it (III.v). This technique, which gave the action in certain scenes the air of being almost simultaneous, was believed to alleviate the static or disconnected quality complained of in sequential performances. Eugen Kilian, who saw this production and reported it in *Shakespeare Jahrbuch,* believed that *Timon* has serious weaknesses, but considered the performance in Munich a success:

> The performance in Munich showed clearly that even this, the most bitter and most brittle of Shakespeare's tragedies, in spite of its unevenness in value,

really can be produced with honour to the German stage, and holds an unlearned public.[52]

In 1950, *Timon* was produced at Dusseldorf, but in Wieland's rather than in a modern prose translation, the interest in the play being "historical rather than intrinsic." The play was again produced successfully by Fritz Kortner at the Kammerspiele, Munich, in 1963, as a symbolic drama.[53]

Performances of *Timon* "in modern dress"—pronounced successful by reviewers but not repeated—have been presented at Yale (1941), at Birmingham, England (1947), and at the Byron Theater, New York (1954), "with exciting contemporary meaning."[54] The Birmingham performance was privately produced by Sir Barry Jackson and staged by the Birmingham Theatre Company for the benefit of delegates to the 1947 Shakespeare Conference. Although the play was found to gain enormously from performance in modern dress, certain serious difficulties in production were experienced. The problem appeared to be a disparity between the "first movement"—essentially "a tragi-comedy of manners"—and the "second movement"—the indictment of man as a social animal. The "second movement"—though ranking at its best moments with the Prometheus of Aeschylus or Shelley—is "closet drama." The Birmingham group found that this second part did not even evoke pity, because pity was "shouted down with wrath." The characterization of Apemantus was difficult because his warped body and mind were more amusing to an Elizabethan audience, presumably, than to an audience in the twentieth century.[55]

In 1952, 1956, and 1958, professional performances of *Timon* were produced by the Old Vic. Between May 28 and June 28, 1952, the play was staged in London at

the Vic with André Morell as Timon. The company
then went to Zurich, where the production was chosen
as the English play in a program entitled, "Shakespeare
in Four Languages."[56] Again in 1956, the Old Vic produced *Timon,* opening the season with the play, with
Sir Ralph Richardson in the title role. The sluggish
nature of the action in the second half of the play was
again observed, as it had been by the Birmingham
group, but it was attributed to Richardson's acting
rather than to the play itself. A reviewer for *Shakespeare Quarterly* commented on Richardson's portrayal
of Timon:

> He understands the outburst of rage that concludes
> the third act, which he let fly with tremendous force.
> But he simply cannot bring himself to believe in the
> last two acts. On his own view of life, generosity,
> tolerance, a sweet reasonableness, and a natural phi-
> lanthropy will keep breaking in.[57]

Two years later, Richardson was again featured in
the title role. According to a reviewer for *Shakespeare
Survey,* Richardson played Timon "too near the middle of the road throughout." The reviewer felt that the
role of Timon calls for a display of active magnanim-
ity in the first part of the play and active agony in
the second part. The reviewer concedes, however, that
there can be little audience identification with Timon,
since "modern middle-class audiences have been indoc-
trinated with ideals of inflation and a credit squeeze."[58]

The "success" of the play is difficult to evaluate
when it is produced by academic groups where performances are partially subsidized, or expenses, at least,
minimal. In 1953, Antioch performed *Timon* successfully in the "Greek and Roman" cycle at the second
annual Shakespeare Festival.[59] In 1955, *Timon* was

attempted in a Shakespearean Festival in Ashland, Oregon, "partly as a labor of love and partly because of a sense of obligation in finishing out the canon." The producers were surprised to find that public interest in this "Shakespearian collector's item" guaranteed "very good houses" and "Both audiences and cast were gratified by the superior quality of the production and its warm reception."[60]

The play was performed five times between May 3 and May 13, 1950, by La Societé génevoise des Amis de l'Instruction, composed of gifted amateurs and professionals. "Though that bitter and imperfect tragedy had been translated before, it had never been acted anywhere in French-speaking countries."[61] The play was performed in a new translation by Daniel Auer, and scored "a real success." Auer attempted "a sort of compromise between the requirements of a modern and those of an Elizabethan stage."

The paradox of *Timon* in the history of the theater is that the play could be so highly admired by such experts in dramaturgy as Garrick, Schiller, and Kean, and yet be so disappointing on the professional stage. One may suspect that the challenge of conveying the extraordinary range of emotions in the play is so intriguing that the difficulties in staging are lost sight of. With the breakdown of emphasis on structure and the growing importance of dramatic texture and of ideas in drama, the future of *Timon* is somewhat more hopeful than past experience with the play would suggest. Yet it seems dubious that *Timon* can ever "hold an unlearned public," as Eugen Kilian predicted.[62] Even the admirers of *Timon* as an experimental form—Collins, Alexander, and Honigmann—have seen the play as originally designed for an academic audience, and certainly, as still appealing to the intellect rather than to the emotions.

Their judgment would be borne out, in general, by the comments of reviewers of *Timon* on the evening of April 8, 1964, on the occasion of the production of the play by the Stratford, Ontario, Company at the Chichester (England) Festival Theatre. Since the play was produced for the Shakespearean quadcentenary year, it was rather fully reviewed by critics for the leading journals. Again, it is interesting to note that critics who reveal a consciousness of structure tend to have a negative reaction to the play in contrast to critics primarily or exclusively concerned with meaning.

For instance, aware of structural difficulties, a critic for the *Evening News*, London, observes:

> While the first part strikes home—the banqueting scene with tired businessmen twisting with hostesses is magnificent—the second part, with Timon in the wilderness, comes properly to life only after his death.

Similarly, after deploring the "shortage of any true dramatic impulse and of any really sustained poetry" in the play, a critic for the *Financial Times,* London writes:

> Timon himself is what current American slang calls a "patsey," a character who is too big a fool to maintain our interest when all goes well with him, and too sorry a spectacle to engage our sympathy when all goes ill.

In contrast to this unfavorable criticism, a critic for the *Scotsman,* Edinburgh, stresses the modern significance of this "racy" production:

> If such things as the Elizabethan system of patronage are not illuminated by the way in which the discussion between the Poet and Painter is handled at the play's opening, the production does not miss the

play's main point—the corruption of a civilization through greed and ingratitude in a degree impossible for one man to bear.

In the *Daily Worker*, London, a critic pronounces the performance "a triumph." He recalls Marx's fascination with the play:

> 'How excellently Shakespeare describes the essence of money,' he [Marx] wrote. 'It was capable of turning everything into its opposite. It is the universal whore, the universal procurer of human beings and peoples.'[63]

A correspondent at Chichester for the *Times*, London, writes optimistically of the play's contemporary meaning:

> Like *Measure for Measure* and *Troilus and Cressida*, it belongs to that harsh section of the Shakespeare canon that modern audiences respond to with so much more instinctive sympathy than their grandfathers did. If this is because dramatic expression of disillusion and cynicism is better understood today, then *Timon of Athens*, most disillusioned and cynical of Shakespeare's plays, is also most of and for today.

As audiences gradually become more familiar with the play, its popularity may increase. In 1963, Norman Sanders pointed out in *Shakespeare Survey* that "a breakdown of the list of plays performed between 1945 and 1960 [at the Royal Shakespeare Theatre] suggests that the overruling factor in attracting audiences has been the long established familiarity of individual plays. During these fifteen years all the plays in the canon have been produced, with the exception of the *Comedy of Errors, Timon of Athens,* and the three parts of *Henry VI*."[64]

Almost immediately thereafter, the process of familiarizing audiences with *Timon* began with the production of the play by the Royal Shakespeare Theatre in the summer of 1965. Popular criticism of this production suggests the variety of opinion still extant as to the meaning of the play. A critic for the London *Observer,* for instance (July 4, 1965), argues amusingly that Timon's misanthropy is "superficial" because the ingratitude which he experiences is shown merely by "people who came to his parties" rather than by members of his own family. (Apparently to that critic, the principle of ingratitude is inoperative outside the family circle!)

But Norman Sanders reports that this production of the play, directed by John Schlesinger with Paul Scofield as Timon, "was a brilliant *tour de force,* and certainly the outstanding production of the season. Peter Hall's *Hamlet* (with David Warner in the lead) created more fuss, but the *Timon* was the more satisfying theatre, and it was (strangely enough) a popular success."[65] Whatever meaning audiences may have derived from the play, *Timon* as theater seems, from the report of this trained and perceptive viewer, to have come into its own.

FOOTNOTES

1. Thomas Shadwell, *Timon of Athens or the Man-Hater* (London, 1678).
2. Gerard Langbaine, *An Account of the English Dramatick Poets* (Oxford, 1691), p. 451.
3. *Ibid.*
4. *Ibid.,* p. 443.
5. Charles Gildon, "Remarks on the Plays of Shakespear," in *The Works of William Shakespear,* ed. Nicholas Rowe (London, 1710), VIII, 373.
6. Robert Gould, *The Play-House, a Satyr* (In *Poems chiefly consisting of Satyrs and Satyrical Epistles* [London, 1689]).
7. *The Works of William Cowper, with a Life of the Author by the editor,* ed. Robert Southey (London, 1854), I, 293.

8. *Ibid.*, pp. 293–294.

9. Thomas Marc Parrott, *The Problem of* Timon of Athens (London, 1923), pp. 3–4.

10. *Op. cit.* "To the Most Illustrious Prince George Duke of Buckingham, &c. I am now to present your Grace with this History of *Timon,* which you were pleased to tell me you liked, and it is more worthy of you, since it has the inimitable hand of *Shakespear* in it, which never made more Masterly Strokes than in this. Yet I can truly say, I have made it into a Play."

11. Shadwell (London, 1678). Shakespeare's and Shadwell's plays are printed on opposite pages in *The Bankside-Restoration Shakespeare,* eds. Appleton Morgan and Willis Vickery. *The Life of Timon of Athens,* I (New York, 1907).

12. For instance, Parrott, *op. cit.,* p. 14.

13. See, for instance, *The Plays of William Shakespeare,* ed. Samuel Johnson (London, 1765), VI, 198.

14. Parrott, *op. cit.,* p. 11.

15. *Timon of Athens,* Arden edition, ed. H. J. Oliver (London, 1959), pp. xxvi–xxvii.

16. Pope, in fact, rejects the passage as spurious. See *The Works of Shakespear,* ed. Alexander Pope (London, 1725), V, 83–84.

17. *Ibid.,* p. 56.

18. Johnson, *op. cit.,* p. 231.

19. Albert S. Borgman, *Thomas Shadwell: His Life and Comedies* (New York, 1928), pp. 49–50.

20. *Ibid.,* pp. 59–60.

21. *Ibid.,* pp. 53–54; 82–83.

22. *Ibid.,* pp. 105–106.

23. Beginning with the Elizabethan period, Parliament sometimes was called the "Aeropagus," in imitation of the Greek place for meetings of government. Milton's *Areopagitica,* for instance, was addressed to Parliament thirty-four years before the publication of Shadwell's play.

24. [John Kelly], *Timon in Love: or, the Innocent Theft . . . As it is acted at the Theatre-Royal in Drury-Lane* (London, 1733).

25. Delisle de la Drévetière, *Timon le Misantrope: Comédie en trois actes précédée d'un prologue.* Représentée pour la première fois, au Théâtre-Italien (Paris, 1722).

26. Kelly, *op. cit.,* in the "Prologue spoken by Mr. Bridgwater."

27. Kelly, *op. cit.,* p. 18.

28. See, for instance, Oliver, *op. cit.,* pp. 152–153.

29. James Love [James Dance], *Timon of Athens. As it is acted at the Theatre-Royal on Richmond-Green. Altered from Shakespear and Shadwell* (London, 1768).

30. *Ibid.,* p. 100.

31. Charles Beecher Hogan, *Shakespeare in the Theatre, 1701–1800* (Oxford, 1952), II, 655.

32. George Winchester Stone, Jr., "Garrick's Handling of Shakespeare's Plays and His Influence upon the Changed Attitude of Shakespearian Criticism during the Eighteenth Century." Unpubl. Diss. (Harvard, 1938), p. 314.

33. *Ibid.*

34. *Ibid.*

35. *Ibid.*

36. *Ibid.*

37. *Ibid.*

38. Hogan, *op. cit.*, pp. 654–655.

39. Richard Cumberland, *Timons of Athens, altered. A tragedy. As it is enacted at the Theatre-Royal in Drury-Lane* (London, 1771), p. 62.

40. *Leigh Hunt's Dramatic Criticism, 1808–1831,* eds. Lawrence Huston Houtchens and Carolyn Washburn Houtchens (New York, 1949), p. 134.

41. *Ibid.*, pp. 134–139.

42. *Ibid.*, p. 134.

43. *Ibid.*, pp. 134–135.

44. *Ibid.*, p. 135.

45. August Fresenius, "Shakespeare's *Timon von Athen* auf der Bühne," *Shakespeare Jahrbuch* (1895), XXXI, 86–87.

46. Eugen Kilian, "*Timon von Athen* auf der heutigen Bühne," *Shakespeare Jahrbuch* (1913), XLIX, 123.

47. *Ibid.*, p. 123. "Unsere Schaubühne hat noch eine grosse Eroberung ausstehen, von deren Wichtigkeit erst der Erfolg sprechen wird. Shakespeares 'Timon von Athen' ist soweit ich mich besinnen kann, noch auf keiner deutschen Bühne erschienen, und, so gewiss ich den Menschen vor allem anderen zuerst in Shakespeare aufsuche, so gewiss weiss ich im ganzen Shakespeare kein Stück, wo er wahrhaftiger vor mir stände, wo er lauter und beredter zu meinem Herzen spräche, wo ich mehr Lebensweisheit lernte, als im 'Timon von Athen'. Es ist wahres Verdienst um die Kunst, dieser Goldader nachzugraben."

48. *Ibid.*, p. 124.

49. *Ibid.*, pp. 125–126.

50. Fresenius (1895), XXXI, *op. cit.*, pp. 82, 110.

51. Kilian (1913), XLIX, *op. cit.*, p. 129.

52. *Ibid.*, p. 136. "Die Aufführung des Stückes in München hat deutlich gezeigt, dass auch diese, die herbste und sprödeste unter Shakespeares Tragödien, trotz ihrer offenbaren Mängel und des ungleichen Wertes ihrer einzelnen Teile, mit Ehren auf der heutigen Bühne zu bestehen und selbst ein ungelehrtes Publikum zu fesseln vermag."

53. "International Notes," *Shakespeare Survey,* 4 (1951), 127, and "International Notes," *Shakespeare Survey,* 16 (1963), 134.

54. Thomas C. Kemp, *The Birmingham Repertory Theatre* (Birmingham, Eng., 1948), pp. 134–135; "Current Theater Notes," *SQ* (1955), VI, 86.

55. Kemp, *op. cit.,* pp. 134–135.

56. "Current Theater Notes," *SQ* (1953), IV, 74.

57. Clare Byrne, "The Shakespeare Season . . . at the Old Vic, 1956–1957," *SQ* (1957), VIII, 466–467.

58. Roy Walker, "Unto Caesar: A Review of Recent Productions," *Shakespeare Survey,* 11, (1958), 131.

59. "Current Theater Notes," *SQ* (1954), V, 67.

60. Horace W. Robinson, "Shakespeare, Ashland, Oregon," *SQ* (1955), VI, 450.

61. "International Notes," *Shakespeare Survey,* 5 (1952), 115.

62. Kilian, *op. cit.,* p. 136.

63. In his *Economic and Philosophical Manuscripts* (1844), Marx quotes from *Timon,* IV.iii.26–44 ("Gold? . . .Do thy right nature."), and observes:

> Money, since it has the *property* of purchasing everything, of appropriating objects to itself, is therefore the *object par excellence.* The universal character of this *property* corresponds to the omnipotence of money, which is regarded as an omnipotent essence . . . money is the *pander* between need and object, between human life and the means of subsistence. But *that which* mediates my life, mediates also the existence of other men for me. It is for me the *other* person. . . .
>
> Shakespeare attributes to money two qualities:
>
> 1. It is the visible deity, the transformation of all human and natural qualities into their opposite, the universal confusion and inversion of things; it brings incompatibles into fraternity.
>
> 2. It is the universal whore, the universal pander between men and nations.
>
> The power to confuse and invert all human and natural qualities, to bring about fraternization of incompatibles, the *divine power* of money, resides in its *essence* as the alienated and exteriorized species-life of men. It is the alienated *power of humanity.*
>
> What I as a *man* am unable to do, what therefore all my individual faculties are unable to do, is made possible for me by means of *money.* Money therefore turns each of these faculties into something which in itself it is not, into its *opposite.*
>
> *Marx-Engels, Gesamtausgabe,* I, 3, 145–146, trans. in Karl Marx, *Selected Writings in Sociology and Social Philosophy,* eds. T. B. Bottomore and Maximilian Rubel, trans. by T. B. Bottomore (London, 1956), pp. 172–173.

64. Norman Sanders, "The Popularity of Shakespeare. . . . ," *Shakespeare Survey,* 16 (Cambridge, 1963), 21.

65. Letter to the author from Norman Sanders, October 10, 1965.

Part Four

SYNTHESIS

IX

Epitaph: *The Synthesis of Structure and Meaning*

You shall see him a palm in Athens again,
and flourish with the highest. (V.i)

THE literary history of *Timon of Athens* has paralleled in its ups and downs the progress of Timon himself in the play. *Timon* was at the top of Fortune's mount among critics of the late seventeenth century. Drake, Gould, and Gildon wrote briefly but favorably of the meaning of the play. Shadwell, damned for his perversion of meaning by Gould and Gildon, had quietly but drastically changed the structure of the play and created a stage success. Shadwell's version, or its adaptations by Love or by Cumberland, continued to attract audiences on occasion from 1678 to 1783, or for more than one hundred years.

But in 1765, Samuel Johnson's edition of Shakespeare's plays appeared, with Johnson's influential criticism. Johnson wrote that *Timon* had "not much art" in its plan or structure, and his interpretation of the meaning of the play—that it was "a powerful lesson against ostentatious liberality"—damned the protagonist. This tragic flaw evoked no pity. Beginning with Johnson's criticism, *Timon* began to fall in critical esteem, very few critics in the eighteenth century, except Malone, Ritson, and Mason, "accompanying his declining foot." By 1839, the awkwardness of the structure had led Charles Knight to decide that Shakespeare could not be wholly responsible for the play. Among the Romantic critics, Ulrici, Hazlitt, and Lamb, who regarded meaning rather than form as the primary prerequisite of art, *Timon* found loyal friends, but their moment passed.

The negative criticism of the structure of *Timon* continued and grew in severity as part of the revolt against Romantic criticism in the late nineteenth century. Finally, on the assumption that such incoherencies in structure could not possibly produce coherent meaning, critics did not look beyond the structural difficulties in the play. In the writings of Fleay, Wright, Robertson, and Sykes, the divided-authorship idea about *Timon* changed from theory to fact. In the criticism of Elmer Stoll, Tucker Brooke, Hardin Craig, and Peter Ure, *Timon* reached "the base o' th' mount."

But while *Timon* is still "in the woods"—still in a maze of adverse criticism—the play has also found fortune again in the image studies. Whatever the final critical evaluation of the merit of image studies may be, they have performed an important function for *Timon:* that of beginning the process of looking for positive qualities in the play instead of tearing it apart to prove that "non-Shakespearean" writing coincides with incoherencies in structure.

The strictures on form in art had begun to loosen during the Romantic period. Closet drama was quite acceptable. Meaning was of first importance. *Timon* was a fascinating study of idealism. By the mid-twentieth century, some critics denied altogether the importance of structure in the play. A. S. Collins wrote of the insignificance in connection with *Timon* of "mere plot." Timon's negation of all values coincided with ideas expressed by some existentialists and some exponents of relativism in art. Walter Kaufmann praised *Timon* in *From Shakespeare to Existentialism*. In *Pale Fire,* Vladimir Nabokov used a quotation from *Timon*—"The Moones an arrant Theefe,/And her pale fire, she snatches from the Sunne"—to build his thesis of the episodic nature of the reality we create through thoughts reflected haphazardly from one to another. Finally, Timon could stand apart "in his naked power and majesty" and say to those "perpetuall sober Gods," the critics:

> My long sicknesse
> Of Health, and Living, now begins to mend,
> And nothing brings me all things.

(V.i.189–191)

Among the critics of *Timon,* there have been flattering friends (G. Wilson Knight—"There is no tragic movement . . . so terrible in all Shakespeare"), and there have been cynical Apemantuses (Hardin Craig—*Timon* "belongs to the region of satire and still more to the region of tirade. Hospitality and liberality are golden virtues, men are too base to appreciate them, shame on them!"). There have been arguments over details (Malone, Deighton—the varying number of talents has no significance; Robertson—the varying number of talents proves that Chapman wrote the play; Oliver—the varying number of talents "clinches" the argument that the play was left unfinished by Shakespeare.) There have been arguments over major points, as the following table will show:

Structure
Excellent: Hazlitt (Romantic); A. S. Collins (mid-20th century)
Poor: Johnson (18th century); Bradley (early 20th century)

Characterization
Excellent: Gildon (17th century); Sisson (mid-20th century)
Poor: Hallam (19th century); Hardin Craig (mid-20th century)

Meaning
Rich: Gould (17th century); Ellis-Fermor (mid-20th century)
Trite: Duport (19th century); Stoll (early 20th century)

Shakespeare Left the Play Unfinished
Yes: Ulrici (Romantic); E. K. Chambers (mid-20th century)
No: C. Knight (Romantic); Honigmann (mid-20th century)

Shakespeare Wrote the Play
Yes: Langbaine (17th century); Kittredge (mid-20th century)
No: White (19th century) (part only); Tucker Brooke (mid-20th century) (part only)

The Play Is a Failure
Yes: Campbell (19th century); Peter Ure (mid-20th century)
No: Drake (17th century); Schiller (early Romantic)

In general, as the above table may serve to indicate, the seventeenth-century, Romantic, and mid-twentieth-century critics like *Timon,* and the eighteenth-, mid- and late nineteenth-century, and early twentieth-century critics do not like the play. How can critical attitudes toward the play be precisely opposite one another? The obvious answer is that two different sets of critical standards are being used to judge the play. Critics with high regard for the importance of structure in art began the study of the play with the study of its structure. They then either (a) flatly stated that Shakespeare had written a clumsy play or (b) tried to explain the puzzling inconsistencies in structure by suggesting that the play was the composite work of two or more writers. Convinced that the play lacked an ordered interconnection of its parts, they assumed that the meaning could not be otherwise than incoherent, and either did not pursue their study of the play beyond the structure, or, if they did, expressed disappointment with the vagaries of meaning. These critics included the neoclassicists and later critics who retained the conviction of the need for an objective consideration of form in art.

On the other hand, critics who regarded the meaning as of prime importance in creative work studied the meaning of the play first. In order to understand the meaning, they tended either (a) to pay no attention at all to structure (b) to minimize its problems by suggesting that Shakespeare left the play unfinished, or (c) to praise the structure as an outgrowth of the meaning, an experimental form beautifully shaped to contain the thought. These critics included a few late seventeenth-century critics, the Romantics, and mid-twentieth-century critics primarily interested in the theme of the play.

The dramatic experience with the play validates the literary experience. Structurally, the play has been generally judged unsatisfactory, both as a literary work and as a stage play. But when emphasis is transferred to meaning, both literary and drama critics find the play of some interest. Because of the slackening demands for form and the increased concern with intellectual texture, the future of *Timon,* I believe, is likely to be somewhat brighter than its past.

My own feelings about the play are that Shakespeare has attempted something unusual in it—the dramatization of an issue which is universal and consequently larger than characterization. Unfortunately, modernization of society has not yet evolved to a point where most people and their various spokesmen can be entertained by a dramatization of issues. Since this play is concerned with the true measure of man, can one expect that the issue will be interesting to the kinds of people who can sympathetically identify with Ann Frank but are unmoved by the issue involved in the slaughter of six million Jews?

Of more immediate import, with whom, in *Timon,* can audiences (or critics) identify? With Timon, who appears good but stupid? Or with his friends? (For in them rather than in the servant, the cynic, and the general, does the action truly center.) Unable to rest in either identity, we too often are like test animals when neither door leads to the cheese. We are irritated. Our criticism is tinged with ill-concealed emotion. If only, we think, Timon had saved that gold he found in the woods, gone back to Athens like a good boy, acknowledged that everyone has his faults, and learned to budget his money!

My observation of the criticism of *Timon* has led me to believe that the audience is a part of the cast—a menacing part. Shakespeare is asking, how does the idealist fit into society? Not only Timon's friends but most other people, too, answer that question: they eject him. Yet I have known some superior men who are fond of the play. I suspect it is one test of character.

Part Five

APPENDICES

A.

Sources

O PINIONS about the source of *Timon of Athens* are as varied as those about the intention, the literary merit, the authorship, or the date of composition of the play. Interest in the source, however, has been greater in the eighteenth and twentieth centuries than in the nineteenth century. During the nineteenth century, editors were interested primarily in the authorship.

Critics believe that the play is derived either (1) directly from Lucian, or from the anonymous *Timon* comedy written in English and based on Lucian, or from Italian or French works derived from Lucian; or (2) from North's translation of Plutarch's "Life of Marcus Antonius;" or (3) from a combination of Lucian and Plutarch and perhaps other sources; or (4) from a lost play.

Perhaps because Lucian is the oldest extant classical source for the Timon story, editors in the eighteenth century reflected their own classical predilections by assuming that Shakespeare had used Lucian as his source. Charles Gildon (1710) states, "This play is plainly taken from Lucian's Timon, and I wonder that Shakespear rather chose to give Roman names to his persons. . . ."[1] On the final page of Pope's edition of *Timon,* Pope adds the note, *"The hint of part of this play taken from* Lucian's *Dialogue* of Timon."[2] Warburton traces the character of Apemantus to Lucian,[3] and Hanmer quotes Warburton and follows Pope in attributing the source of the play to Lucian.[4] The chain of ascriptions to Lucian breaks down in the nineteenth century, although the influence of Lucian on the play is noted by Hudson (1851)[5] and White (1875).[6] In the 1905 Arden edition of *Timon,* K. Deighton draws specific parallels between Lucian's *Dialogue* and Shakespeare's play.[7]

Based on Lucian, the anonymous Timon comedy in manuscript form, in English, is seen by some critics as a principal source for Shakespeare's *Timon.* Although Alexander Dyce, who edited the anonymous Timon comedy in 1842, could see no resemblance between that play and Shakespeare's *Timon* and although he doubted whether Shakespeare ever saw the manuscript play, a few critics believe that they have discovered parallels between the two plays. W. H. Clemons writes:

> The academic play alone actually introduced Timon in his period of prosperity, its Laches is the only known predecessor of Flavius and of all the extant sources, it is unique in containing a banquet scene.[8]

Robert Goldsmith finds that "a network of correspondences" ties together not only Shakespeare's play and the old Timon but *King Lear* as well.[9]

Some critics believe that Lucian's version reached Shakespeare through Italian or French sources. R. W.

Bond finds parallels between Shakespeare's *Timon* and Boiardo's *Timone,* a five-act play well known in Italy one hundred years before Shakespeare's play was written.[10] The danger, of course, in proving sources by parallel phrasing is that it is difficult to rule out coincidence—any two writers writing on the same subject are likely to have similar thoughts and express them in a similar way. Because of the lack of overall resemblance between Boiardo's and Shakespeare's plays, critics have been hesitant to accept Bond's parallels— Georges Bonnard writing, for instance, that "R. W. Bond ne nous paraît pas avoir prouvé l'influence directe sur Shakespeare."[11] The possibility of Shakespeare's use of a French translation of Lucian in shaping his play has been suggested by E. A. J. Honigmann, who lists parallels between certain passages in Shakespeare's play and passages in Filbert Bretin's translation of *Les Oeuvres de Lucian* (1562).[12]

Those who stress Plutarch rather than Lucian as the main source for Shakespeare's *Timon* point out that while preparing to write *Antony and Cleopatra,* Shakespeare quite likely would have read the story of Timon in the "Life of Marcus Antonius" in North's translation of Plutarch. North's Plutarch as the source for *Timon* is suggested by Edmond Malone in his "Attempt to ascertain the Order" of Shakespeare's plays.[13] (Most critics since Malone tend to think that Shakespeare's *Timon* came either from a variety of sources or from a lost play.) Tucker Brooke finds that "the theme seems to have come to Shakespeare's notice in Plutarch's Life of Antony."[14] Hardin Craig accepts Plutarch as the main source.[15] Robert Law has strengthened the argument for Plutarch as a main source in observing that "Of the nineteen names in *Timon of Athens,* eighteen are in Plutarch."[16]

Among those who see in several sources the raw material combined in Shakespeare's *Timon* are Maxwell, Kittredge, Sisson, Farnham, and Oliver. The combined sources are principally Lucian, the anonymous *Timon* comedy, and Plutarch, or works derived from Plutarch. Kittredge finds that Shakespeare drew both from Lucian and Plutarch for the play.[17] Maxwell finds "little substance" in Kittredge's suggestions that the behavior of Apemantus in Act I owes something to the cynic Alcidamus in Lucian's *Symposium,* and that the crime of the unknown soldier in the Alcibiades-Senate scene in Act III recalls the murder of Phrynichus, in Plutarch's *"Life of Alcibiades".*[18] Maxwell sees the sources of the play as Plutarch, Lucian, and the anonymous *Timon.*[19] He does not quarrel with Kittredge's general ascriptions of sources in the play in Acts IV and V. According to Kittredge:

> From Lucian came Timon's discovery of gold and the return of the parasites, whom Timon drives away with blows; also the visit of the Senators, with their promise of "special dignities." From Plutarch are taken Timon's death, his burial (V.i.219 ff.) and the epitaphs.[20]

Sisson agrees with Kittredge that threads from both Plutarch and Lucian are "woven together" in the play.[21]

Willard Farnham gives the most detailed account of the strains in various versions of the story of Timon which may have merged in Shakespeare's play.[22] Concentrating on the development of the beast theme in the play, Farnham finds traces of the influence of both Lucian and Plutarch. From Lucian, Farnham believes, comes Timon's passing mention of wolves and also the references to the flatterers as "beasts of prey" or "birds of prey." The beast theme is elaborated in Painter's account "Of the strange and beastlie Nature of *Timon of Athens*"—Painter's account being a blend of Plutarch and Claude Gruget. Pedro Mexia's Spanish version had been the source of Gruget's story, which in turn was retold in an improved version by Boaistuau and translated into English by John Alday *ca.* 1566. Further improvements were added by Alday in his *Theatrum Mundi* (1581). This background of variations on the beast theme contributes to the richness of the beast symbolism in Shakespeare's *Timon*. Farnham finds that Shakespeare enlarged on these sources to such an extent that human society in the play appears to have "more of beasthood than of manhood."[23]

H. J. Oliver, editor of the new Arden edition of *Timon*, believes "That Shakespeare's main source for the story of Timon was North's Plutarch," and that rather than being an alternative to North, Painter was only a possible supplementary source: "Painter omitted facts which Shakespeare knew from North."[24] Oliver also sees a slight influence of Lucian on Shakespeare's *Timon:*

> If Shakespeare had somewhat vague memories of Lucian studied at school some twenty-five years before and only in a Latin translation, then I can well believe that his play would have exactly the kind of distant relationship with the original Greek that *Timon of Athens* has.[25]

Oliver finds, too, that the plot of the old Timon comedy written in English and based on Lucian "is certainly closer to Shakespeare's than is Lucian's."[26] But Oliver thinks that it is difficult to understand how Shakespeare could have known this pedantic play, still in manuscript. Oliver leans toward accepting a suggestion of Bonnard's—that Shakespeare's play derives from a lost

prose or play version of the Timon story,[27] something
with a similar relationship to Shakespeare's play as
Whetstone's *Promos and Cassandra* has to *Measure for
Measure*. "Perhaps," writes Oliver, "some such source
will one day be found."

The idea of an older play on which Shakespeare's
play is based is not new. Some nineteenth-century editors postulate the existence of such a play in connection
with their theory of the divided authorship of *Timon*.
Charles Knight suspects "that *Timon of Athens* was a
play originally produced by an artist very inferior to
Shakspere, and which probably retained possession of
the stage for some time in its first form."[28] Of Shakespeare's *Timon*, Verplanck is of the opinion that "Shakespeare engrafted it upon the feebler Timon of a feebler
drama, that held possession of the stage."[29] Comparing
Shakespeare's *Timon* with the old Timon comedy,
Staunton writes:

> These resemblances are no doubt merely owing to
> both plays being founded on a common origin; for
> the subject was evidently familiar to the stage long be-
> fore we can suppose Shakespeare to have produced his
> version.[30]

The emphasis, however, has been primarily on finding
skeletal remains of the *ur*-play in Shakespeare's *Timon*—
the effort of Charles Knight and some of the other divided-authorship theorists—rather than on looking for
the source itself.

Many of the possible source studies are still undeveloped. A study could be made, for instance, of the
elements of the morality in *Timon* in possible relationship to similar elements in the late moralities on
money problems—*Enough Is as Good as a Feast, The*

Trial of Treasure, and *All for Money.* The relationship, if any, should be determined between Shakespeare's *Timon* and his admirer's, Richard Barnfield's,
The Encomion of Lady Pecunia.[31]
Since the action of the entire play is foreshadowed
in the striking image of Fortune on a hilltop, something
more definite about the source of *Timon* might be
learned from tracking this particular depiction of Fortune to the tapestry, game, emblem, ballad, or literary
work where it may originate. Described as "well-worn"
by some critics of Timon,[32] Shakespeare's depiction of
Fortune is quite different actually from the usual images
of Fortune on an island, turning a wheel, sitting on a
wheel, etc.[33] In view of the beast imagery throughout
the play[34] the relation of Fortune to the Roman Fortuna—"Our Lady of Beasts"—and the Circe archetype
from which she descends certainly should be explored.

Whatever discoveries are made about the source of
the play, however, the editorial opinions that Shakespeare drew most of the story from a combination of
Lucian and Plutarch are unlikely to require revision.

FOOTNOTES

1. Charles Gildon, "Remarks on the Plays of Shakespear,"
The Works of Mr. William Shakespear, ed. Nicholas Rowe (London, 1710), VII, 373.
2. *The Works of Shakespear,* ed. Alexander Pope (London,
1725), V, 5.
3. *The Works of Shakespear,* ed. William Warburton (London, 1747), VI, 172.
4. *The Works of Shakespear,* ed. Sir Thomas Hanmer (Oxford, 1744), VI, 155.
5. *The Works of Shakespeare,* ed. H. N. Hudson (Boston and
Cambridge, 1855), VIII, 9.
6. *The Works of William Shakespeare,* ed. Richard Grant
White (Boston, 1875), X, 198.

7. *Timon of Athens,* The Arden Shakespeare, ed. K. Deighton (London, 1905), pp. xxvii–xxx.

8. W. H. Clemons, *The Sources of* Timon of Athens, *Princeton Univ. Bull.* (1903–1904), XV, 217.

9. Robert Hillis Goldsmith, "Did Shakespeare Use the Old Timon Comedy?" *SQ* (1958), IX, 32.

10. Matheo Maria Boiardo, *Comedia del Timone. traducto de uno dialogo de Luciano* (Venice, 1517).

11. Georges A. Bonnard, "Note sur Les Sources de *Timon of Athens,*" *Études Anglaises* (January, 1954), VII, 69.

12. E. A. J. Honigmann, "Timon of Athens," *SQ* (1961), XII, 8–11.

13. *The Plays and Poems of William Shakespeare,* ed. Edmond Malone (London, 1790), I, 372.

14. Tucker Brooke, *The Literary History of England,* ed. Albert C. Baugh (New York, 1948), p. 539.

15. *A History of English Literature,* ed. Hardin Craig (New York, 1950), p. 268.

16. Robert Adger Law, "On Certain Proper Names in Shakespeare," *SQ* (1953), IV, 352.

17. *The Complete Works of Shakespeare,* ed. George Lyman Kittredge (New York, 1936), p. 1045.

18. *Timon of Athens,* ed. J. C. Maxwell (Cambridge, Eng., 1957), pp. xxi–xxii.

19. *Ibid.,* p. xxi.

20. Kittredge, *op. cit.,* p. 1045.

21. *William Shakespeare: The Complete Works,* ed. Charles Jasper Sisson (London, 1954), p. 910.

22. Willard Farnham, *Shakespeare's Tragic Frontier: The World of His Final Tragedies* (Berkeley and Los Angeles, 1950), pp. 39–72.

23. *Ibid.,* p. 68.

24. *Timon of Athens,* Arden edition, ed. H. J. Oliver (London, 1959), p. xxxiii.

25. *Ibid.,* p. xxxvii.

26. *Ibid.,* p. xxxviii.

27. *Ibid.,* p. xl, and Georges A. Bonnard, "Note sur Les Sources de *Timon of Athens,*" *Études Anglaises* (January, 1954), XII, 59–69.

28. *The Pictorial Edition of the Works of Shakspere,* ed. Charles Knight (London, 1839), V, 333.

29. *Shakespeare's Plays,* ed. Gulian C. Verplanck (New York, 1847), III, 6.

30. *The Plays of Shakespeare,* ed. Howard Staunton (London, 1859), II, 459.

31. Richard Barnfield, *The Encomion of Lady Pecunia or the Praise of Money* (London, 1596).

32. Maxwell, *op. cit.*, p. xxxi.

33. Howard Rollin Patch, "The Tradition of the Goddess Fortuna in Roman Literature and in the Traditional Period," *Smith Coll. Studies in Modern Languages*, III, No. 3 (April, 1922); III, No. 4 (June, 1922).

34. Erich Neuman, *The Great Mother: An Analysis of the Archetype*, trans. Ralph Manheim (New York, 1955), p. 273 and Fig. 62.

B.

DATING

CRITICS disagree as to when *Timon of Athens* was written. A few believe that the play belongs to the end of the Elizabethan period, or *ca.* 1602. Others see it as following the "problem" plays, *Troilus* and *Measure for Measure.* They believe that *Timon* was written between 1605 and 1608. Some critics think that Shakespeare wrote the play at the end of his career, that is, *ca.* 1610 or later.

Theories as to the date of the play are based on its subject matter and/or style. Representative of critics who favor the early date is Nathan Drake, who conjectures that *Timon* was written in 1602, shortly after the academic *Timon* play, which Drake assumes was written in the late sixteenth century.[1] In Drake's opinion, Shakespeare's interest in a play exploring the humor of the malcontent was stimulated by the production of Jonson's *Every Man Out of His Humour* (1599). Dixon Wecter, who thinks he sees in the character of Timon resemblances to the Earl of Essex, also believes that the play was written in the Elizabethan period, shortly after Essex's tragic death. (In his edition of *Timon,* Samuel Johnson had noted a marked resemblance between Essex's remarks in a letter and Timon's noble rebuke of Apemantus in Act IV.[2]) Wecter and Paul Jorgensen believe that the play as Shakespeare wrote it at the end of the Elizabethan period was mutilated subsequently to hide references to Essex.[3]

Several critics who place *Timon* in the late middle period of Shakespeare's career as a playwright see it as following *Lear.* Coleridge associates the play with *Lear* in theme, but makes no attempt to determine when *Timon* was written.[4] Quoting Coleridge in connection with his conjecture as to the play's date, Julian Verplanck places it "as of the epoch of *Measure for Measure,* the revised *Hamlet,* and *Lear."* Frederick Gard Fleay assigns *Timon* the date of 1606 "between *Lear* and the later Roman plays."[5] His judgment is based on "the texture of the diction,—which is about midway between the mellow, gliding smoothness of the Poet's second period, and the stern, rugged energy of his last. . . ." Una Ellis-Fermor also believes that *Timon* belongs to the period in which *Lear* was written. She finds a sequence in theme in which *Macbeth* and *Lear* lead up to *Timon.* "Timon defines the theme that *Lear* had touched."[6] Whereas Miss Ellis-Fermor regards *Timon* as representing a stage in the development of Shakespeare's ideas, Hardin Craig looks on the play as exemplifying a stage in the development of Shakespeare's style: "In style the play is late, but possibly not much later than *King Lear.*"[7]

While ascribing *Timon* to the same period assigned it by Verplanck, Fleay, Miss Ellis-Fermor, and Hardin Craig, some critics are inclined to emphasize its closeness in time to *Antony and Cleopatra.* According to Kittredge, "tests of mood, style, and metre might put it anywhere from 1605 to 1608. . . . The subject of Timon may have impressed itself on Shakespeare's mind when he was reading Plutarch with a view to his *Antony and Cleopatra.*"[8] In view of "its powerful, compressed style," Charles Sisson dates *Timon* "at a late period of Shakespeare's writing, but before the new manner and atmosphere of his latest plays during the years of his close study of Plutarch for dramatic purposes and near to the years of *Coriolanus* and *Antony and Cleopatra.*"[9] James McManaway writes that "lacking objective evidence, commentators agree on a date between 1605 and 1608.[10]

A still later date for the composition of *Timon* was suggested by Edmond Malone, the first editor to show an intensive interest in the chronology of Shakespeare's plays. In his "Attempt to ascertain the Order in which the Plays of Shakspeare were written," Malone conjectures that *Timon* was written *ca.* 1610.[11] He chooses this date because "Most of his *other* plays have been attributed, on plausible grounds at least, to *former years;*" and because Shakespeare would have come across the subject of *Timon* while studying the life of Antony in Plutarch *(Antony and Cleopatra* was entered for publication in the *Stationers Register* in 1608). To reinforce his theory about the date of the play, Malone comments that the plagues of 1593 and 1603 undoubtedly made a deep impression on Shakespeare, but that the frequent mentions of plague in *Timon* were perhaps stimulated by "the more immediate recollection of the plague which raged in 1609." Hermann Ulrici would also give the play a late date. On the basis of its style, he declares that it is "unquestionably one of the last tragedies of our poet, in all likelihood, the very last."[12]

The trend toward seeing *Timon* as a social problem play following *Troilus* (Alexander, Harold Wilson, Honigmann) supports Kittredge's conjecture that the play belongs to the period between 1605 and 1608.

FOOTNOTES

1. Nathan Drake, *Shakspeare and His Times* (London, 1817), II, 447.

2. Dixon Wecter, "Shakespeare's Purpose in *Timon of Athens*," *PMLA* (1928), XLIII, 704, 720.

3. Paul A. Jorgensen, *Shakespeare's Military World* (Berkeley and Los Angeles, 1956), pp. 267, 279.

4. Samuel Taylor Coleridge, *Lectures and Notes on Shakespeare and Other Dramatists*, World's Classics, Pb. (Oxford, 1931), p. 134.

5. Frederick Gard Fleay, *Shakespeare Manual* (London, 1878), p. 102.

6. Una Ellis-Fermor, *The Jacobean Drama: An Interpretation* (London, 1936), p. 264.

7. Hardin Craig, *An Interpretation of Shakespeare* (New York, 1948), p. 103.

8. *The Complete Works of Shakespeare,* ed. George Lyman Kittredge (Boston, 1936), p. 1046.

9. *William Shakespeare: The Complete Works,* ed. Charles Jasper Sisson (London, 1954), p. 910.

10. James G. McManaway, "Recent Studies in Shakespeare's Chronology," *Shakespeare Survey,* 3 (1950), 30.

11. *The Plays and Poems of William Shakespeare,* ed. Edmond Malone, I, 372–373.

12. Hermann Ulrici, *Shakespeare's Dramatic Art,* trans. Alexander J. W. Morrison (London, 1846), p. 238.

BIBLIOGRAPHY

1.

EDITIONS

ALEXANDER, PETER, ed. *The Works of William Shakespeare*. New York, 1952.

BOSWELL, JAMES AND EDMOND MALONE, eds. *The Plays and Poems of William Shakespeare*. 21 vols. London, 1821.

CAPELL, EDWARD, ed. *Mr. William Shakespeare Comedies, Histories, and Tragedies*. 10 vols. London, 1767–1768.

CLARK, WILLIAM GEORGE AND WILLIAM ALDIS WRIGHT, eds. *The Works of William Shakespeare*. The Globe edition. London, 1864.

———. *The Works of William Shakespeare*. Cambridge edition. 9 vols. London, 1863–1866.

COLLIER, J. PAYNE, ed. *The Works of William Shakespeare*. 8 vols. London, 1842.

CRAIG, W. J., ed. *The Complete Works*. The Oxford Shakespeare. London, 1905.

DEIGHTON, K., ed. *Timon of Athens*. The Arden Shakespeare. London, 1905.

DYCE, ALEXANDER, ed. *The Works of Shakespeare*. 6 vols. London, 1857.

———. *The Works of William Shakespeare*. 9 vols. London, 1864–1867.

EVANS, H. A., ed. *The Henry Irving Shakespeare. Timon of Athens*. New York, 1888–1890.

FARMER, RICHARD, ed. *The Plays of William Shakespeare*. 12 vols. London, 1800.

Folio editions.
[First Folio]. *Shakespeares comedies, histories, & tragedies; being a reproduction in facsimile of the first folio edition, 1623, from the Chatsworth copy in the possession of the Duke of Devonshire, K. G., with introduction and census of copies by Sidney Lee.* Oxford, 1902.
[Second Folio]. *Mr. William Shakespeare Comedies, Histories, and Tragedies, Published according to the true Originall Copies.* The second impression. London, 1632.
[Third Folio]. *(Mr. William Shakespear's) comedies, histories, and tragedies, faithfully reproduced in facsimile from the edition of 1664.* London, Methuen and Co., 1905.
[Fourth Folio]. *Mr. William Shakespear's Comedies, histories, and tragedies. Published according to the true original copies. Unto which is added, seven plays, never before printed in folio.* Fourth edition. London, 1685.
GOLLANCZ, ISRAEL, ed. *The Temple Shakespeare.* 40 vols. London, 1899–1902.
HANMER, SIR THOMAS. *The Works of Shakespear.* 6 vols. Oxford, 1744–1746.
HUDSON, H. N., ed. *The Works of Shakespeare.* 11 vols. Cambridge, Mass., 1851–1856.
———. *The Works of Shakespeare.* 11 vols. Boston, 1872.
———. *The Complete Works of William Shakespeare.* Harvard edition. 20 vols. Boston, 1881.
JOHNSON, SAMUEL, ed. *The Plays of William Shakespeare.* 8 vols. London, 1765.
———, GEORGE STEEVENS, AND ISAAC REED, eds. *The Plays of William Shakespeare.* 10 vols. London, 1785.
———. *The Plays of William Shakespeare.* 15 vols. London, 1793.
KITTREDGE, GEORGE LYMAN, ed. *The Complete Works of Shakespeare.* New York, 1936.
KNIGHT, CHARLES, ed. *The Pictorial Edition of the Works of Shakspere.* 8 vols. London, 1838–1843.
MALONE, EDMOND, ed. *The Plays and Poems of William Shakespeare.* 10 vols. London, 1790.
MAXWELL, J. C., ed. *The Life of Timon of Athens.* Cambridge, 1957.
OLIVER, H. J., ed. *Timon of Athens.* The Arden edition. London, 1959.
POPE, ALEXANDER, ed. *The Works of Shakespear.* 6 vols. London, 1723–1725.
RIDLEY, M. R., ed. *Timon of Athens.* The New Temple Shakespeare. London, 1934.
ROLFE, WILLIAM J., ed. *Timon of Athens.* New York, 1895.
———. *Timon of Athens.* New York, 1906.

Rowe, Nicholas, ed. *The Works of Mr. William Shakespear.* 6 vols. London, 1709–1710.

Singer, Samuel Weller, ed. *The Dramatic Works of William Shakspere.* 10 vols. Cheswick, 1826.

Sisson, C. J., ed. *William Shakespeare The Complete Works.* London, 1954.

Staunton, Howard, ed. *The Plays of Shakespeare.* 3 vols. London, 1858–1860.

Theobald, Lewis, ed. *The Works of William Shakespeare.* 7 vols. London, 1733.

Verplanck, Gulian C., ed. *Shakespeare's Plays.* 3 vols. New York, 1847.

Warburton, William, ed. *The Works of William Shakespear.* 8 vols. London, 1747.

White, Richard Grant, ed. *The Works of William Shakespeare.* 12 vols. Boston, 1875.

——. *Mr. William Shakespeare's Comedies Histories Tragedies and Poems.* Riverside edition. 6 vols. Boston, 1883.

Williams, Stanley T., ed. *The Life of Timon of Athens.* The Yale Shakespeare. New Haven, 1919.

2.

GENERAL REFERENCES: *Prior to 1800*

Barnfield, Richard. *The Encomion of Lady Pecunia or the Praise of Money.* London, 1596.

Boiardo, Matheo Maria. *Comedia del Timone. traducto de uno dialogo de Luciano.* Venice, 1517.

Cotgrave, John. *The English Treasury of Wit and Language. Collected Out of the most, and best of our English Dramatick Poems.* London, 1655.

Cumberland, Richard. *Timon of Athens, altered. A tragedy. As it is enacted at the Theatre-Royal in Drury-Lane.* London, 1771.

Drake, James. *The Antient and Modern Stages survey'd, or Mr Collier's View of the Immorality and Profaness of the English Stage Set in a True Light.* London, 1699.

Drévetière, Delisle de la. *Timon le Misantrope. Comédie en trois actes précédée d'un prologue.* Paris, 1722.

[Edwards, Thomas]. *A Supplement to Mr Warburton's Edition of Shakespear. Being the canons of Criticism and Glossary, Collected from the Notes in that celebrated Work, And proper to be bound up with it.* By another Gentleman of Lincoln's Inn. Second edition. London, 1748.

Fortune—The boke of the fayre Gentylwoman that no man shulde put in his truste—that is to say, Lady Fortune. London, 1554.

GILDON, CHARLES. "Remarks on the Plays of Shakespear." *The Works of Mr. William Shakespear*, ed. Nicholas Rowe. vol. VII, London, 1710, 372–376.

GOULD, ROBERT. *Poems Chiefly consisting of Satyrs and Satyrical Epistles.* London, 1689. [Containing *The Play-House. a Satyr. Writ in the Year 1685.*]

[GREY, ZACHARY]. *An Examination of a Late Edition of Shakespear: wherein Several Plagiarisms are taken Notice of, and the late Sir Tho. Hanmer, Bart. vindicated. Addressed to the Reverend Mr Warburton, Preacher of Lincoln's Inn, By a Country Gentleman.* London, 1752.

———. *Critical, Historical, and Explanatory Notes on Shakespeare, with Emendations of the Text and Metre.* 2 vols. London, 1754.

Heath, Benjamin. *A Revisal of Shakespear's Text, wherin the Alterations introduced into it by the more modern Editors and Critics, are particularly considered.* London, 1765.

[Kelly, John]. *Timon in Love: or, the Innocent Theft, A comedy taken from Thimon Misanthrope of the Sieur de Lisle. As it is Acted at the Theatre-Royal in Drury-Lane.* London, 1733.

LANGBAINE, GERARD. *An Account of the English Dramatick Poets.* Oxford, 1691.

LOVE, JAMES. [JAMES DANCE]. *Timon of Athens. As it is acted at the Theatre-Royal on Richmond-Green. Altered from Shakespear and Shadwell.* London, 1768.

MASON, JOHN MONCK. *Comments on the Last Edition of Shakespeare's Plays.* Dublin, 1785.

RICHARDSON, WILLIAM. *Essays on Shakespeare's Dramatic Characters,* 2nd. ed. (London, 1785).

RITSON, JOSEPH. *Remarks Critical and Illustrative, on the Text and Notes of the Last Edition of Shakespeare.* London, 1783.

SHADWELL, THOMAS. *Timon of Athens or the Man-Hater.* London, 1678.

THEOBALD, LEWIS. *Shakespeare restored: or, a Specimen of the Many Errors, as well Committed, as Unamended, by Mr. Pope In his Late Edition of this Poet.* London, 1726.

UPTON, JOHN. *Critical Observations on Shakespeare.* London, 1746.

3.
GENERAL REFERENCES AFTER 1800: *Books or Monographs*

ALEXANDER, PETER. *Shakespeare's Life and Art.* New York, 1961. (First edition, 1939.)

BABB, LAWRENCE. *The Elizabethan Malady: A Study of Melancholia in English Literature from 1580 to 1642.* East Lansing, 1951.

BAUGH, ALBERT C., ed. *A Literary History of England.* New York, 1948.

BORGMAN, ALBERT S. *Thomas Shadwell His Life and Comedies.* New York, 1948.

BRADLEY, A. C. *Shakespearean Tragedy.* London, 1904.

BRUCKNER, FERDINAND [THEODORE TAGGER]. *Timon Tragödie,* Berlin, 1932.

CAMPBELL, O. J. *Shakespeare's Satire.* New York, 1943.

CAMPBELL, THOMAS, et al., eds. *Lives of the British Dramatists.* Philadelphia, 1846.

CAZAMIAN, LOUIS. *L'Humour de Shakespeare.* Paris, 1945.

CHAMBERS, E. K. *William Shakespeare: A Study of Facts and Problems.* Oxford, 1930.

——, *Shakespeare: A Survey.* London, 1948.

CLEMEN, WOLFGANG. *The Development of Shakespeare's Imagery.* New York, 1961. (Revised English edition, Cambridge, Mass., 1951, based on *Shakespeare's Bilder.* Bonn, 1936.)

CLEMONS, W. H. *The Sources of Timon of Athens. Princeton Univ. Bull.* IV. 1903–1904.

COLERIDGE, SAMUEL TAYLOR. *Lectures and Notes on Shakespeare and Other Dramatists.* World's Classics, Pb. Oxford, 1931.

CRAIG, HARDIN, ed. *A History of English Literature.* New York, 1950.

——. *An Interpretation of Shakespeare.* New York, 1948.

DANBY, JOHN F. *Poets on Fortune's Hill.* Studies in Sidney, Shakespeare, Beaumont and Fletcher. London, 1952.

DODD, WILLIAM. *The Beauties of Shakspeare.* London, 1825. (Previously printed in 1752, 1757, and 1780.)

DORAN, MADELEINE. *Endeavors of Art: A Study of Form in Elizabethan Drama.* Madison, 1954.

DOWDEN, EDWARD. *Shakspere His Mind and Art.* New York and London, 1902.

DRAKE, NATHAN. *Shakspeare and His Times.* 2 vols. London, 1817.

DUNN, E. CATHERINE. *The Concept of Ingratitude in Renaissance English Moral Philosophy.* Unpubl. Diss. Catholic University. Washington, 1946.

DUPORT, PAUL. *Essais Littéraires sur Shakspeare.* 2 vols. Paris, 1828.

DYCE, ALEXANDER, ed. *Timon.* (The old Timon mss. play.) London, 1842.

ELLIS-FERMOR, UNA. *The Frontiers of Drama.* New York, 1946.

——. *The Jacobean Drama: An Interpretation.* London, 1936.

——. *Some Recent Research in Shakespeare's Imagery.* Shakespeare Assn. Papers. London, 1937.

ELWIN, W. AND W. J. COURTHOPE, eds. *The Works of Alexander Pope.* 10 vols. London, 1871–1889.

EMPSON, WILLIAM. *The Structure of Complex Words.* London, 1951.

FARNHAM, WILLARD. *Shakespeare's Tragic Frontier: The World of His Final Tragedies.* Berkeley and Los Angeles, 1950.

FLEAY, FREDERICK GARD. *Shakespeare Manual.* London, 1878.

FLUCHÈRE, HENRI. *Shakespeare.* trans. by Guy Hamilton. London, 1953.

GREEN, HENRY. *Shakespeare and the Emblem Writers.* London, 1870.

GREG, W. W. *The Editorial Problem in Shakespeare.* Oxford, 1942.

————. *The Shakespeare First Folio.* Oxford, 1955.

HALLAM, HENRY. *Introduction to the Literature of Europe.* 4 vols. London, 1837.

HOGAN, CHARLES BEECHER. *Shakespeare in the Theatre 1701–1800.* 2 vols. Oxford, 1952.

HOLLOWAY, JOHN. *The Story of the Night.* London, 1961.

HOUTCHENS, LAWRENCE HUSTON AND CAROLYN WASHBURN HOUTCHENS, eds. *Leigh Hunt's Dramatic Criticism, 1808–1831.* New York, 1949.

HOWE, P. P., ed. *The Complete Works of William Hazlitt.* 21 vols. London, 1930.

HUDSON, H. N. *Lectures on Shakespeare.* 2 vols. New York, 1848.

HUTCHINSON, THOMAS, ed. *The Works of Charles and Mary Lamb.* Oxford, 1924. (First edition, 1908.)

JORGENSEN, PAUL A. *Shakespeare's Military World.* Berkeley and Los Angeles, 1956.

KAUFMANN, WALTER. *From Shakespeare to Existentialism.* New York, 1960.

KEMP, THOMAS C. *The Birmingham Repertory Theatre.* Birmingham, Eng., 1948.

KNIGHT, G. WILSON. *The Wheel of Fire.* London, 1930.

LANGBAUM, ROBERT. *The Poetry of Experience.* New York, 1957.

MORGAN, APPLETON AND WILLIS VICKERY, eds. *The Bankside-Restoration Shakespeare.* 5 vols. New York, 1907.

MURRY, JOHN MIDDLETON. *Shakespeare.* London, 1936.

NABOKOV, VLADIMIR. *Pale Fire.* New York, 1962.

NEUMAN, ERICH. *The Great Mother: An Analysis of the Archetype.* trans. by Ralph Manheim. New York, 1955.

PARKER, MARION D. HOPE. *The Slave of Life: A Study of Shakespeare and the Idea of Justice.* London, 1955.

PARROTT, THOMAS MARC. *The Problem of* Timon of Athens. Shakespeare Assn. Papers, No. 10, London, 1923.

RIBNER, IRVING. *Patterns in Shakespearian Tragedy.* New York, 1960.

ROBERTSON, J. M. *Shakespeare and Chapman.* London, 1917.
SCHELLING, FELIX E. *Elizabethan Drama: 1558–1642.* 2 vols. New York, 1959. (First edition, 1910.)
SCHLEGEL, A. W. *Lectures on Dramatic Art and Literature.* trans. by John Black, London, 1846.
SOUTHEY, ROBERT, ed. *The Works of William Cowper, with a Life of the Author by the editor.* 8 vols. London, 1854.
SPURGEON, CAROLINE. *Shakespeare's Imagery and What It Tells Us.* Cambridge, Eng., 1935.
STOLL, ELMER EDGAR. *Art and Artifice in Shakespeare.* Cambridge, Eng., 1933.
———. *Shakespeare and Other Masters.* Cambridge, Mass., 1940.
STONE, GEORGE WINCHESTER, JR. *Garrick's Handling of Shakespeare's Plays and His Influence upon the Changed Attitude of Shakespearian Criticism during the Eighteenth Century.* Unpubl. Diss., Harvard, 1938.
SWINBURNE, ALGERNON CHARLES. *A Study of Shakespeare.* New York, 1880.
SYKES, H. DUGDALE. *Sidelights on Elizabethan Drama.* Oxford, 1924.
TENNYSON, ALFRED. *Poetic and Dramatic Works.* Cambridge, Mass., 1898.
TRAVERSI, D. A., *An Approach to Shakespeare.* New York, 1956. (First edition, 1938.)
ULRICI, HERMANN. *Shakespeare's Dramatic Art.* trans. by Alexander J. W. Morrison, London, 1846.
URE, PETER. *Shakespeare: The Problem Plays.* London, 1961.
VAN DOREN, MARK. *Shakespeare.* New York, 1939.
WHITE, RICHARD GRANT. *Studies in Shakespeare.* Boston, 1899.
WILSON, F. P. *Elizabethan and Jacobean.* Oxford, 1946.
WILSON, HAROLD S. *On the Design of Shakespearian Tragedy.* Toronto, 1957.
WRIGHT, ERNEST HUNTER. *The Authorship of Timon of Athens.* New York, 1910.

4.
GENERAL REFERENCES: *Periodicals*

ALEXANDER, PETER. "Restoring Shakespeare: The Modern Editor's Task," *Shakespeare Survey,* 5 (1952), 1–9.
ALEXANDER, PETER. "Troilus and Cressida, 1609," *Library,* IX (1928), 267–286.
BENTLEY, GERALD EADES. "John Cotgrave's *English Treasury of Wit and Language* . . .," *SP,* XL (April 2, 1943), 186–203.
BOND, R. W. "Lucian and Boidardo in *Timon of Athens,*" *MLR,* XXVI (1931), 52–68.

BONNARD, GEORGES A. "Note sur Les Sources de *Timon of Athens,*" *Études Anglaises,* VII (January, 1954), 59–69.

BYRNE, CLARE. "The Shakespeare Season . . . at the Old Vic, 1956–1957," *SQ,* VIII (1957), 466–467.

CHAMBERS, E. K. "The Disintegration of Shakespeare," *Proceedings, Br. Acad.* XI (1924–1925), 89–108.

COLLINS, A. S. "*Timon of Athens:* A Reconsideration," *RES,* XXII (April, 1946), 96–108.

COOK, DAVID. "Timon of Athens," *Shakespeare Survey,* 16 (1963), 83–94.

"CURRENT THEATER NOTES," *SQ,* IV (1953), 61–75.

———. *SQ,* V (1954), 51–69.

DRAPER, J. W. "The Theme of *Timon of Athens,*" *MLR,* XXIX (1934), 20–31.

DRAPER, R. P. "*Timon of Athens,*" *SQ,* VIII (1957), 195–200.

ELLIS-FERMOR, UNA. "*Timon of Athens:* An Unfinished Play," *RES,* XVIII (July, 1942), 270–283.

FRESENIUS, AUGUST. "Shakespeare's *Timon von Athen* auf der Bühne," *Shakespeare Jahrbuch,* XXXI (1895), 82–125.

GOLDSMITH, ROBERT HILLIS. "Did Shakespeare Use the Old Timon Comedy?" *SQ,* IX (1958), 31–38.

HONIGMANN, E. A. J. "*Timon of Athens,*" *SQ,* XII (1961), 3–20.

"INTERNATIONAL NOTES," *Shakespeare Survey,* 4 (1951), 123–126; *Shakespeare Survey,* 16 (1963), 134.

KILIAN, EUGEN. "*Timon von Athen* auf der heutigen Bühne," *Shakespeare Jahrbuch,* XLIX (1913), 122–136.

LAW, ROBERT ADGER. "On Certain Proper Names in Shakespeare," *Univ. of Texas Studies in Eng.,* XXX (1951), 257.

McMANAWAY, JAMES G. "Recent Studies in Shakespeare's Chronology," *Shakespeare Survey,* 3 (1950), 22–33.

MERCHANT, W. M. "*Timon* and the Conceit of Art," *SQ,* VI (1953), 249–257.

NOWOTTNY, WINIFRED M. T. "Acts IV and V of *Timon of Athens,*" *SQ,* X, No. 4 (1959), 493–497.

OLIVER, H. J. "Review of *Timon of Athens,* ed. by J. C. Maxwell," *SQ,* IX (1958), 406–407.

PAULIN, BERNARD. "La Mort de Timon d'Athènes," *Études Anglaises,* XVII, No. 1. (1964), 8.

PATCH, HOWARD ROLLIN. "The Tradition of the Goddess Fortuna in Roman Literature and in the Traditional Period," *Smith Coll. Studies in Modern Languages,* III, No. 3 (April, 1922); III, No. 4 (June, 1922).

SANDERS, NORMAN. "The Popularity of Shakespeare: An Examination of the Royal Shakespeare Theatre's Repertory," *Shakespeare Survey,* 16 (1963), 18–29.

SPENCER, TERENCE. "Shakespeare Learns the Value of Money: The Dramatist at Work on *Timon of Athens*," *Shakespeare Survey*, 6 (1953), 75–78.

WALKER, ROY. "Unto Caesar: A Review of Recent Productions," *Shakespeare Survey*, 11 (1958), 128–135.

WECTER, DIXON. "Shakepeare's Purpose in *Timon of Athens*," *PMLA*, XLIII (1928), 701–721.

WENDLANDT, WILHELM. "Shakespeare's *Timon von Athen*," *Shakespeare Jahrbuch*, XXIII (1888), 107–192.

WILLIAMS, PHILIP, JR. "New Approaches to Textual Problems in Shakespeare," *Studies in Bibliography*, VIII (1956), 8–14.

WILSON, F. P., "Shakespeare and the Diction of Common Life," *Proceedings, Br. Acad.*, XXVII (London, 1944), 167–197.

INDEX

Alexander, Peter, 49, 64, 66, 102–4, 106–7, 111, 144, 173
Amorous Bigotte, The (Shadwell), 130
An Account of the English Dramatick Poets (Langbaine), 4, 120
Anacreon, 111
Anatomy of Melancholy, The (Burton), 106
Antient and Modern Stages survey'd, The (James Drake), 90
Areopagus, 131
Aristotle, 13–14, 59–60, 88, 107
Art and Artifice in Shakespeare (Stoll), 14
Auden, W. H. *(passim)*, 105
Auer, Daniel, 119, 144
Authorship of Timon of Athens, The (E. H. Wright), 42

B

Babb, Lawrence, 76

Bacon, Francis *(passim)*, 105
Barnfield, Richard, 167
Bentley, Gerald Eades, 90
Boiardo, Matheo Maria, 163
Bond, R. W., 162–63
Bonnard, Georges A., 163, 165–66
Borgman, Albert S., 147
Boswell, James (Third Variorum), 10
Bradley, A. C., 24, 156
Brave New World (Huxley), 72
Bretin, Filbert, 163
Brooke, Tucker, 39, 56, 154, 156, 163
Bulwer-Lytton, Edward, 84
Burton, Robert, 106
Byrne, Clare, 143

C

Campbell, Thomas, 86, 156
Capell, Edward, 6, 8–10, 29
Cazamian, Louis, 88–89
Chambers, E. K., 28, 31, 36, 38, 46, 48–50, 52, 54–56, 156

Chapman, George, 29, 34–37, 54, 94, 121, 155
Characters of Shakespeare's Plays (Hazlitt), 63
Charney, Maurice, 57, 96
Clark, William George and William Aldis Wright, 20–21, 41
Clemen, Wolfgang, 98–99
Clemons, W. H., 162
Coleridge, Samuel Taylor, 87–88, 109, 171
Collier, J. Payne, 45–46, 96
Collins, A. S., 64–65, 102–7, 111, 113, 144, 155–56
Cook, David, 89
Cormier, Ramona T., 51
Cotgrave, John, 76
Craig, Hardin, 36, 39, 55–56, 88–89, 113, 154–56, 163, 171
Crane, Ralph, 68–69
Cumberland, Richard, 119, 121, 134–37, 140–41, 153

D

Daily Worker (London), 146
Dance, James (James Love), 121, 134, 153
Davies, Thomas, 136
Day, John 37–38, 94
Deighton, K., 22–23, 30–31, 155, 162
Dennis, John *(passim)*, 124
Dodd, William, 76
Doran, Madeleine, 76
Dowden, Edward, 24
Drake, James, 76, 153, 156
Drake, Nathan, 76, 78, 170
Draper, J. W., 99–100
Draper, R. P., 100
Drévetière, Delisle de la, 133, 148
Dryden, John, 129
Duchess of Malfi (Dutchess of Malfy), 28
Duport, Paul, 13–14, 156

Dyce, Alexander, 17–18; ed. old Timon comedy, 17–18, 47, 162, 164–66

E

Editorial Problem in Shakespeare, The (Greg), 53
Elizabethan and Jacobean (F. P. Wilson), 55
Ellis-Fermor, Una, 50–51, 54, 64, 80, 100, 102–4, 106–7, 111, 156, 171
Empson, William, 101
Endeavors of Art: A Study of Form in Elizabethan Drama (Doran), 91
English Treasury of Wit and Language, The (Cotgrave), 90
Essais Littéraires sur Shakspeare (Duport), 13
Essex, Earl of, 170–71
Études Anglaises, 92, 168
Evans, H. A., 21, 79
Evening News (London), 145
Every Man Out of His Humour (Jonson), 170
Examiner (Hunt's criticism in), 137–39

F

Farnham, Willard, 80, 101, 164–65
Financial Times (London), 145
Fleay, Frederick Gard, 24, 26–28, 30–31, 33–34, 39–41, 67–69, 154, 171
Fluchère, Henri, 105–7
Folio (1623), 4, 6, 22, 29, 44, 68, 70
Fortune (archetype), 167
Fresenius, August, 140–41
From Shakespeare to Existentialism (Kaufmann), 109–10, 155

G

Garrick, David, 121, 134–36, 144
Gascoigne, George, 18
Gildon, Charles, 60, 62–63, 76, 120, 140, 153, 156, 162
Goldsmith, Robert Hillis, 162
Gollancz, Israel, 22, 39–41, 49
Gould, Robert, 95, 120–21, 153, 156
Greg, W. W., 52–53, 67–68, 70

H

Hall, Joseph, 18
Hallam, Henry, 55, 76, 78–79, 156
Hanmer, Sir Thomas, 7–8, 96, 162
Hazlitt, William, 62–64, 80, 82, 100, 104, 139, 154, 156
Heywood, Thomas, 18
Holloway, John, 101
Honigmann, E. A. J., 64, 66–70, 102, 107, 109, 111, 113, 144, 156, 163, 173
Horace, 135
Hudson, H. N., 18–19, 39–41, 46, 55, 79, 81, 162
Hull, Thomas, 121, 134
Humour out of Breath (Day), 37–38
Hunt, Leigh, 80, 137–39
Huxley, Aldous, 71–72

I

"I.H.," 130
Inns-of-Court, 66–67, 70, 109
Introduction to the Literature of Europe (Henry Hallam), 55

J

Jenkins, Harold, 66, 106
Johnson, Samuel, 8–10, 12, 15, 18–21, 23, 26, 31–32, 38, 45–46, 61–62, 64, 76–78, 80, 82, 96, 125–26, 138, 153, 156, 171
Jonson, Ben, 66, 88, 170
Jorgensen, Paul A., 76, 171

K

Kaufmann, Walter, 102, 109–11, 155
Kean, Edmund, 137, 144
Kelly, John, 133
Kilian, Eugen, 141, 144, 156
Kittredge, George Lyman, 51–52, 156, 164, 172–73
Knight, Charles, 15–20, 26–27, 39–41, 45, 49, 52, 79–81, 96, 154, 156, 166
Knight, G. Wilson, 80, 85–86, 155

L

Lamb, Charles, 80, 82–83, 103, 154
Lamb, George, 119, 137, 141
Lancashire Witches, The (Shadwell), 130
Langbaine, Gerard, 4, 120, 156
Langbaum, Robert, 86
Law, Robert Adger, 163
Les Oeuvres de Lucian (Bretin), 163
Library, 72
Literary History of England, A, 56
Locke, John, 96
Love, James (James Dance), 121, 134, 137, 153
Lucian, 30, 35, 47, 70, 101, 133, 161–65, 167

M

Macflecknoe (Dryden), 129
McManaway, James G., 172
Malcontent, The (Marston), 66
Malone, Edmond, 10, 29–30, **61**, 76, 78, 154–55, 163, 172

Marston, John, 18, 67
Marx, Karl, 146
Mason, John Monck, 61–62, 154
Maxwell, J. C., 53–54, 102, 111, 164
Merchant, W. M., 76
Middleton, Thomas, 37–38, 94
Modern Language Review (MLR), 114
Molière, Jean-Baptiste *(passim)*, 104
Murphy, Arthur, 136
Murry, John Middleton, 76

N
Nabokov, Vladimir, 111–12, 155
New York Times Book Review Section, 115
North's Plutarch, 52, 161, 163, 165
Nowottny, Winifred M. T., 39

O
Observer (London), 147
Oliver, H. J., 30–31, 36, 49–50, 54–55, 64, 67–71, 96, 102, 108–9, 111, 113, 155, 164–66

P
Painter, William, 101, 164–65
Pale Fire (Nabokov), 111, 155
Parrott, Thomas Marc, 34–37, 39–41, 98, 121–22
Paulin, Bernard, 92
Play-House, The, a Satyr. (Robert Gould), 95, 113
Plutarch, 30, 47, 52, 70, 101, 161, 163–67, 172
Point Counter Point (Huxley), 71
Pope, Alexander, 7–9, 76–77, 125, 129 *(passim)*, 162

Proceedings, Br. Acad., 28, 41, 113
PMLA, 173
Punch, 85

R
Rape of the Lock, The (Pope) *passim,* 129
Reed, Isaac, 10
Rehearsal, The (Villiers), 129
"Remarks on the Plays of Shakespear" (Gildon), 60
"Restoring Shakespeare: The Modern Editor's Task" (Alexander), 49–50
Revenger's Tragedy, The (Tourneur), 28
Review of English Studies, The (RES), 50, 64
Ribner, Irving, 101
Richardson, William, 92
Ridley, M. R., 49, 51–52
Ritson, Joseph, 10, 61, 154
Robertson, J. M., 28–31, 35–36, 54–55, 94, 98, 154–55
Robinson, Horace W., 149
Rolfe, William J., 21–22, 39–41
Ronsard, 111
Rowe, Nicholas, 4–7, 9, 27, 60, 76
Rymer, Thomas *(passim),* 124

S
Sanders, Norman, 147
Saturday Review, The, 113
Schelling, Felix, 24
Schiller, Johann Friedrich, 80, 140–41, 144, 156
Schlegel, A. W., 62–63, 80, 86–87, 89
Scotsman (Edinburgh), 145
Shadwell, Thomas, 15, 53, 119–34, 136, 141, 153; *Amorous Bigotte, The,* 130; *Lancashire*

Witches, The, 130; *Timon of Athens or the Man-Hater,* 119–34, 136

Shaftesbury, Earl of, 130

Shakespeare, William (Plays), *Antony and Cleopatra,* 52, 96, 163, 172; *Comedy of Errors,* 146; *Coriolanus,* 68, 90, 172; *Hamlet,* 106, 110–11, 171, *Henry VI,* 146; *Julius Caesar,* 30; *King Lear,* 56, 81, 85–89, 95, 98, 102, 106, 109, 111, 121, 162, 171; *Macbeth,* 85, 102, 106, 110, 171; *Measure for Measure,* 66, 81, 90, 146, 166, 170–71; *Othello,* 86; *Pericles,* 24, 113; *The Tempest,* 95, 113, 121; *Timon of Athens* (chart of Ascriptions), 39–41; (key scenes in): Alcibiades-Senate, 15–16, 19, 23, 35–36, 38, 46, 50–54, 60, 62–63, 65–66, 101, 105, 123, 140–41; Apemantus-Fool, 5, 8, 15, 19, 38, 50–51, 123; Banquets, 35–36, 53, 122–23, 139, 147; Poet-Painter opening scene, 5, 35–36, 64, 104, 122, 145–46; Poet-Painter visit in woods, 8–10, 15–16, 20, 23, 31–32, 36, 38, 45–46, 51–52, 61–62, 65–66; Soldier in woods, 7, 9, 15, 20–21, 23, 38, 65, 124; (talent argument), 28–31, 35–36, 54–55, 155–56; *Troilus and Cressida,* 53, 66–67, 90, 103, 107, 146, 170, 173; *The Winter's Tale,* 106

Shakespeare Assn. Papers, 34–36, 114, 121–22

Shakespeare First Folio, The (Greg), 53

Shakespeare Jahrbuch, 47–48, 139–42

Shakespeare Manual (Fleay), 27

Shakespeare Quarterly (SQ), 43, 66, 69, 114, 142–46, 168

Shakespeare Survey, 49, 142 46

Shakespearean Tragedy (Bradley), 24

Shakspeare and His Times (Drake), 78

Singer, Samuel Weller, 62, 79–81

Sisson, C. J., 55, 64–66, 102, 106–7, 111, 156, 164, 172

Smith College Studies (Patch), 169

Socrates, 51

Southey, Robert, 80, 120–21

Spencer, Terence, 30

Spurgeon, Caroline, 96–99

"Stage Vindicated, The: A Satyr" ("I.H."), 130

Staunton, Howard, 17, 166

Steevens, George, 10, 16, 29, 76, 78

Stoll, Elmer, 14, 76, 79, 154, 156

Stone, George Winchester, 148

Studies in Bibliography, 68

Studies in Philology (SP), 90

Swinburne, Algernon Charles, 55, 62, 80, 84

Sykes, H. Dugdale, 37–41, 94, 98, 154

T

Tennyson, Alfred, 80, 84–85

Theobald, Lewis, 7

Times (London), 146

Timon (anonymous play, ed. Dyce), 17–18, 47, 162, 164–66

Timon in Love (Kelly), 133

Timon le Misantrope (Drévetière), 148

Timon of Athens or the Man-Hater (Shadwell), 119–34, 136

Timone (Boiardo), 163
Tourneur, Cyril, 27–28
Traversi, D. A., 88

U

Ulrici, Hermann, 45, 48–49, 62,
    80, 83–84, 86, 89, 139, 154,
    156, 172
Ure, Peter, 14, 154, 156

V

Van Doren, Mark, 14, 88
Verplanck, Gulian C., *Frontispiece*, 18, 166, 171
Villiers, George, Duke of Buckingham, 122, 128
Volpone (Jonson), 66

W

Walker, Roy, 143
Warburton, William, 7, 95, 162
Way of the World, The (passim), 113
Webster, John, 28

Wecter, Dixon, 170–71
Wendlandt, Wilhelm, 46–48
Whetstone, George *(passim)*,
    166
White, Richard Grant, 19–20,
    30, 39–41, 79, 81, 156, 162
Whiter, Walter, 96
*William Shakespeare: A Study
    of Facts and Problems*
    (Chambers), 48
Williams, Philip, Jr., 67–69
Williams, Stanley T., 23
Wilson, F. P., 55, 96
Wilson, Harold S., 66, 107–8,
    111, 113, 173
Wilson, J. Dover, 36, 53
Wright, Ernest Hunter, 24, 31–
    34, 37, 39–41, 46, 98, 154

Y

Yeats, William Butler *(passim)*,
    104
Your Five Gallants (Middleton), 37–38